ADVANCED MODULAR MATHEMATICS

Mechanics
2

for A and AS level
The University of London modular mathematics syllabus

Stephen Webb
for

NATIONAL
EXTENSION
COLLEGE

D1412965

Collins Educational
An Imprint of HarperCollinsPublishers

Published by Collins Educational
An imprint of HarperCollins*Publishers*
77–85 Fulham Palace Road
Hammersmith
London W6 8JB

This book was written by Stephen Webb for the National Extension College Trust Ltd.

Designed by Derek Lee
Cover design and implementation by Derek Lee
Page layout by Mary Bishop
Project editor, Hugh Hillyard-Parker

The author and publishers thank Pat Perkins and Trevor Jennings for their comments on this book.

Printed and bound in the UK by Scotprint, Musselburgh

The National Extension College is an educational trust and a registered charity with a distinguished body of trustees. It is an independent, self-financing organisation.

Since it was established in 1963, NEC has pioneered the development of flexible learning for adults. NEC is actively developing innovative materials and systems for distance-learning options from basic skills and general education to degree and professional training.

For further details of NEC resources that support *Advanced Modular Mathematics*, and other NEC courses, contact NEC Customer Services:

National Extension College Trust Ltd
18 Brooklands Avenue
Cambridge CB2 2HN
Telephone 01223 316644, Fax 01223 313586

CONTENTS

M2

Advanced Modular Mathematics

FOREWORD

This book is one of a series covering the University of London Examination and Assessment Council's modular 'A' level Mathematics syllabus. It covers all the subject material for Mechanics 2 (Module M2).

While this series of text books has been structured to match the University of London (ULEAC) syllabuses, we hope that the informal style of the text and approach to important concepts will encourage other readers, whose final examinations are from other examination Boards, to use the books for extra reading and practice.

This book is meant to be *used*: read the text, study the worked examples and work through the exercises, which will give you practice in the basic skills you need for maths at this level. There are many books for advanced mathematics, which include many more exercises: use this book to direct your studies, making use of as many other resources as you can. This book will act as a bridge between your new syllabus and the many older books that can still give even more practice in advanced mathematics.

Exercises are given at the end of each section; these range from the basic to exam-type questions. Many exercises, and worked examples, are based on *applications* of the mathematics in this book. We have given answers to all problems, so that you can check your work.

The National Extension College has more experience of flexible-learning materials than any other body (see p. ii). This series is a distillation of that experience: *Advanced Modular Mathematics* helps to put you in control of your own learning.

M2

Introduction: Modelling

The questions facing you when you sit your exam are likely to include descriptions of situations occuring in the real world which you then have to transform into a mathematical model. In making this transformation, you have to make certain simplifications and assumptions in order to keep the working on a manageable level. You will see that throughout Module M2, many of the topics that you have covered in Module M1 will crop up again with additional features, making the appropriate model a more accurate representation of the actual situation.

The ideal components familiar to you from your work on Module M1 still continue to apply in Module M2 on the whole:

● You will still model people, cars and other objects as **particles**.

● You will be looking at strings which are elastic, but whether elastic or inextensible, strings and ropes are modelled as being **light**, i.e. of negligible weight compared to the object (particle) they are supporting.

● Ladders and planks and anything rigid of this kind are generally modelled as **uniform rods**.

● Many of the surfaces as well as wires, pulleys and hinges are taken to be **perfectly smooth**, so that no friction acts.

● As in Module M1, motion is in general modelled by supposing that there is **no air resistance**. There may be some examples where a constant resistance is taken into account, but we have to wait for Module M3 before we consider a resistance changing with velocity.

Variable acceleration

INTRODUCTION The familiar equations for motion, like $v^2 = u^2 + 2as$, are only true when the acceleration is **constant.** If the acceleration changes in some way we have to use a different method: this usually means the setting up and solving of an appropriate differential equation. In this section we are going to look at the kinds of equations that arise and the techniques we'll need for solving them systematically.

As you work through this section, you may find you need to refresh your memory on the following topics, covered in Modules P1 and P2.

- integration
- differential equations
- properties of natural logarithms
- partial fractions.

If you have not yet covered those parts of Module P2 that deal with differential equations, you may find it advisable to complete this section at a later stage and should start with Section 2 of this module.

Systematic approach

By and large, if we're given the acceleration as a function of another variable (which can be velocity, time or displacement), the method of solution can be broken down into fairly well-defined sections. For the moment we'll make a list of these and then look at each in turn:

1 Sign
2 Form
3 Setting up
4 Integrating
5 Values
6 Rearranging

1st stage: Sign

As in many types of question which deal with **vector** quantities, i.e. where the **direction** is important, we have to choose a positive direction. This often chooses itself – if we are told that a car is moving in a straight line, then obviously we take its direction of motion as positive. There are two cases where you have to be careful, however. If you are told that a force produces a **retardation**, it means that the acceleration will automatically be negative. Alternatively you could be told that a particle is moving in the positive direction of the positive x-axis – if the force on the body is then towards the origin, this will tend to slow the body down and so the acceleration will be negative.

2nd stage: Form

There are two main forms for the acceleration with which you should be familiar.

$$① \; \frac{dv}{dt} \quad \text{and} \quad ② \; v\frac{dv}{dx} \qquad \begin{array}{l} \text{where } v \text{ is the velocity} \\ x \text{ is the displacement} \end{array}$$

If we start from the definition of acceleration, the rate of change of velocity, we have

$$a = \frac{dv}{dt} \qquad \qquad \ldots ①$$

then
$$a = \frac{dv}{dt} = \frac{dv}{dx} \times \frac{dx}{dt} = \frac{dv}{dx} \times v = v\frac{dv}{dx} \qquad \ldots ②$$

(There is a third form, $\frac{d^2x}{dt^2}$, but this is not used so much.)

If we're given the acceleration as:

- a function of t, we use $\dfrac{dv}{dt}$

- a function of x, we use $v\dfrac{dv}{dx}$

- a function of v, we use either form, depending on the question.

3rd stage: Setting up

Having chosen the appropriate form for the acceleration we should have a first-order differential equation with separable variables and we proceed as normal by putting all the terms of one variable on one side and all the terms of the other variable on the other. There are a couple of points here. If you have two (or more) terms added or subtracted on one side, e.g.

$$\frac{dv}{dt} = 3 + v$$

then you have to take **all** of this to join the dv on the other side,

$$\text{i.e.} \int \frac{dv}{3+v} = \int dt$$

and not $\int \frac{dv}{v} = \int 3dt$, a common mistake.

Also, it makes integration easier if you leave any constants **outside** the integral and on the less cluttered side, e.g. to rearrange

$$\frac{dv}{dt} = \frac{-3v}{5},$$

it might be easier to put $\int \frac{dv}{v} = -\frac{3}{5}\int dt$,

rather than $\int \frac{-5dv}{3v} = \int dt$.

4th stage: Integrating

By the very nature of the forms for acceleration, certain types of integral crop up again and again and you have to be able to recognise and carry out the particular one in question. The following are very typical and as a reminder we'll run through them.

| **Example** | Integrate: |

(a) $\displaystyle\int \frac{1}{v - v^2} dv$ (b) $\displaystyle\int \frac{v}{1 + v} dv$ (c) $\displaystyle\int \frac{v}{1 + v^2} dv$

| **Example** | (a) The bottom of the fraction is a quadratic which factorises, and so we use **partial fractions**: |

$$\int \frac{1}{v - v^2} dv = \int \frac{1}{v(1-v)} dv = \int \left(\frac{1}{v} + \frac{1}{1-v}\right) dv$$

$$= \ln|v| - \ln|1-v| + C$$

$$= \ln\left|\frac{v}{1-v}\right| + C$$

(b) The power of the function on the top is the **same** as the power on the bottom, so we have to **divide** first:

$$
\begin{array}{r}
1 \\
v+1 \overline{\smash{\big)}\, v } \\
\underline{v+1} \\
-1
\end{array}
\qquad \Rightarrow \frac{v}{v+1} = 1 - \frac{1}{v+1}
$$

and $\displaystyle\int \frac{v}{1+v} dv = \int \left(1 - \frac{1}{v+1}\right) dv$

$$= v - \ln|v+1| + C$$

3

(c) The top is more or less the **derivative** of the bottom, so the integral is a log function:

$$\int \frac{v}{1 + v^2}\, dv = \frac{1}{2}\int \frac{2v}{1 + v^2}\, dv = \frac{1}{2}\ln(1 + v^2) + C$$

You should now be able to answer Exercise 1 on p. 14.

5th stage: Values

Once we've integrated the equation successfully, we have the **general solution**, i.e. we will have an arbitrary **constant** from the integration. To find the value of this constant we need to know a **pair of values** for the variables in the solution. This pair of values can be written into the question in such a way that they are not immediately obvious, and you have to be able to 'translate' into mathematical symbols. For example:

- 'Initially' means when $t = 0$
- 'Starts from rest' means that $v = 0$ when $t = 0$
- 'Greatest height' means that $v = 0$
- 'Returns to its initial position' means that $x = 0$ (again), and others.

6th stage: Rearranging

Once we've found the solution to the equation, we then have to express it in the required form – since the solution frequently involves ln's, we need to be able to manipulate these. You may already be familiar with this from solving differential equations in Module P2, but as a reminder there are a few general principles and mistakes to avoid.

Gather all the ln's to one side, combine to one ln and then use the fact that $\ln a = b \Rightarrow a = e^b$ to eliminate any ln's.

e.g. $\quad \ln v = 4 - \ln t \Rightarrow \ln v + \ln t = 4$

$\ln vt = 4$

$vt = e^4 \Rightarrow v = \dfrac{e^4}{t} \quad$ (and not $v = e^4 - t$)

When combining ln's, use the property that $n \ln a = \ln a^n$ *first of all*,

e.g. $\quad \ln v + \dfrac{1}{2}\ln(v + 1) = \ln v + \ln(v + 1)^{\frac{1}{2}}$

$= \ln v(v + 1)^{\frac{1}{2}} \quad$ (and not $\dfrac{1}{2}\ln v(v + 1)$)

That then is the sequence of stages through which the solution of a typical problem might pass. It's not intended as a rigid framework and you'll probably find that the question doesn't fit exactly – but on the whole it gives a fair indication of how to proceed. Let's take a question and see it working.

Example

The acceleration of a particle, moving on the positive x-axis, has magnitude $n^2(3a - x)$, where x is the displacement from the origin O and n and a are positive constants. The direction of the acceleration is towards O. At time $t = 0$, the particle is moving through the point $x = a$ with speed $2na$ away from O. Show that, in the ensuing motion, the speed v of the particle is given by:

$$v = n(3a - x)$$

Hence find x in terms of t.

Sketch the graph of x against t.

Solution

Sign: We're told that the direction of the acceleration is 'towards O', so that it is **negative**, of magnitude $n^2(3a - x)$.

Form: Since the acceleration is given in terms of x, we choose the form $v\dfrac{dv}{dx}$.

Setting up: Combining the parts above, we have:

$$v\frac{dv}{dx} = -n^2(3a - x)$$
$$\int v\,dv = \int -n^2(3a - x)dx$$
$$\int v\,dv = -n^2\int (3a - x)dx$$

Integrating: No problem in this example, noting that a is constant, so that $3a$ integrates to $3ax$.

$$\frac{v^2}{2} = -n^2\left(3ax - \frac{x^2}{2}\right) + C \qquad \qquad \text{...①}$$

Values: We're told that when $x = a$, the speed is $2na$ away from O, i.e. positive and $v = 2na$.

Putting these values into equation ①

$$\frac{(2na)^2}{2} = -n^2\left(3a^2 - \frac{a^2}{2}\right) + C$$

$$2n^2a^2 = -\frac{5a^2n^2}{2} + C \implies C = \frac{9a^2n^2}{2}$$

and so $\dfrac{v^2}{2} = -n^2\left(3ax - \dfrac{x^2}{2}\right) + \dfrac{9a^2n^2}{2}$

Rearranging: $\times 2$ $v^2 = -6n^2ax + n^2x^2 + 9a^2n^2$

$$= n^2(9a^2 - 6ax + x^2) = n^2(3a - x)^2$$

Take square roots $\implies v = \pm n(3a - x)$

But we know that $v = 2na$ when $x = a$, so we discard the negative solution and

$$v = n(3a - x)$$

The next part of the question is a little twist – we have to use the fact that $v = \dfrac{dx}{dt}$ and then set up a differential equation in x and t.

$$\frac{dx}{dt} = n(3a - x) \implies \int \frac{dx}{3a - x} = n \int dt$$

$$\implies -\ln(3a - x) = nt + D$$

But we're told that when $t = 0$, $x = a$ and so $-\ln 2a = D$ for $x < 3a$. Putting this back in,

$$-\ln(3a - x) = nt - \ln 2a$$

$$\implies \ln 2a - \ln(3a - x) = nt$$

$$\implies \ln \frac{2a}{3a - x} = nt$$

$$\implies \frac{2a}{3a - x} = e^{nt}$$

$$\implies (3a - x)(e^{nt}) = 2a$$

$$\implies 3a - x = \frac{2a}{e^{nt}} = 2ae^{-nt}$$

$$\implies x = 3a - 2ae^{-nt}$$

Figure 1.1

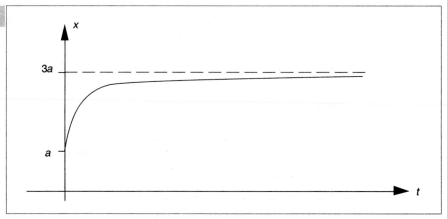

The sketch of this function shows how the distance from O was a when t was 0, and how the distance approaches a **limiting value** of $3a$ as t becomes large and consequently the term $2ae^{-nt}$ becomes very small.

Increases in the variables

We are frequently asked to find the increase in one variable corresponding to the increase in the other – for example, find the time taken for the particle to move from the point where $x = a$ to the point where $x = 3a$. In this case we measure our time **from the first point,** i.e. we let t be zero when $x = a$. When we put this pair of values into our general solution we'll find the value of the arbitrary constant and can find the new value of t when $x = 3a$. Here's an example of this kind where we want to find an increase in **distance** corresponding to a given increase in the speed.

Example

A small smooth sphere S, of mass 0.2 kg, moves in a straight line with variable acceleration $(2 + v)$ m s^{-2}, where v m s^{-1} is the speed of the sphere. Find the distance, to the nearest 0.1 m, moved by S as its speed increases from 1 m s^{-1} to 5 m s^{-1}.

Solution

We have the choice between $\dfrac{dv}{dt}$ or $v\dfrac{dv}{dx}$ for the acceleration, but since the question combines distance with speed, we want $v\dfrac{dv}{dx}$.

$$v\frac{dv}{dx} = 2 + v \quad \Rightarrow \int \frac{v}{2+v}\,dv = \int dx$$

To integrate the LHS, we have to divide through to start with:

$$
\begin{array}{r}
1 \\
v + 2 \overline{)\, v} \\
v + 2 \\
\hline
-2
\end{array}
\qquad \Rightarrow \frac{v}{2+v} = 1 - \frac{2}{v+2}
$$

and our equation becomes:

$$\int\left(1 - \frac{2}{v+2}\right) dv = \int dx \quad \Rightarrow v - 2\ln(v+2) = x + C$$

Now we're going to measure distance from the point where the speed is 1 m s^{-1}, i.e. $x = 0$ when $v = 1$. Putting these values in

$$1 - 2\ln 3 = C$$

and so $v - 2\ln(v+2) = x + 1 - 2\ln 3$

$$\Rightarrow \quad x = v - 1 + 2\ln 3 - 2\ln(v+2)$$

$$= v - 1 + 2\ln\frac{3}{v+2}$$

so when $v = 5$, $x = 5 - 1 + 2\ln\frac{3}{7} = 2.3$ m (1 d.p.)

You should now be able to answer Exercises 2–5 on pp. 14–15.

Variable force

Instead of an acceleration or retardation, we are sometimes given a force which varies with one of velocity, displacement or time. Apart from some preliminary work, the method is the same as the one we have just been using.

We need a connection between the force applied and the acceleration produced – this comes from Newton's Second Law:

> Newton's Second Law: $F = ma$
>
> where F is the force in Newtons,
> m is the mass in kg,
> and a is the acceleration in m s^{-2}.

Since the mass can make the working more complicated, the force will usually be given in such a way that m disappears. This can be done either by giving the force in terms of m or, equivalently, by giving the force **per unit mass**, which means that we have to multiply the force by m, the mass of the particle it is acting on. In both these cases, the same m will appear on both sides of the equation and will cancel.

Remember that any force which **resists** the motion in the positive direction, or **opposes** the motion or is given as a retarding force will be **negative**.

Here's an example where in fact we will use both forms for the acceleration.

| **Example** | At time $t = 0$, a particle of mass m is projected with speed U from the origin and moves along the positive x-axis. The only force acting on the particle is a resistance of magnitude $mk\left(\dfrac{v}{U}\right)^{\frac{3}{2}}$, where v is the speed of the particle and k is a positive constant. Find an expression in terms of U, k and v, for the displacement x of the particle and show that the particle never passes the point where $x = \dfrac{2U^2}{k}$. |

Find an expression for v in terms of U, k and the time t.

| **Solution** | The force is a **resistance** and so it will be negative. |

$$F = -mk\left(\frac{v}{U}\right)^{\frac{3}{2}} \qquad \qquad \text{... ①}$$

and since $F = ma$,

$$ma = -mk\left(\frac{v}{U}\right)^{\frac{3}{2}} \text{ and the } m\text{'s cancel}$$

$$a = -k\left(\frac{v}{U}\right)^{\frac{3}{2}} \qquad \qquad \dots ②$$

We're asked for an expression involving the **distance** and so we'll use $a = v\dfrac{dv}{dx}$ and ② becomes:

$$v\frac{dv}{dx} = -k\left(\frac{v}{U}\right)^{\frac{3}{2}}$$

which rearranges to

$$\int \frac{v\,dv}{v^{\frac{3}{2}}} = \int \frac{-k}{U^{\frac{3}{2}}}\,dx \qquad \qquad \dots ③$$

i.e. $\displaystyle \int \frac{dv}{v^{\frac{1}{2}}} = \frac{-k}{U^{\frac{3}{2}}}\int dx \quad \Rightarrow \quad 2v^{\frac{1}{2}} = \frac{-kx}{U^{\frac{3}{2}}} + C \qquad \dots ④$

At the origin, i.e. $x = 0$, we're told that the speed of the particle was U, i.e. $v = U$. Putting these into ④,

$$2U^{\frac{1}{2}} = C \quad \text{and ④ becomes}$$

$$2v^{\frac{1}{2}} = \frac{-kx}{U^{\frac{3}{2}}} + 2U^{\frac{1}{2}} \quad \text{and rearranging,}$$

$$\frac{kx}{U^{\frac{3}{2}}} = 2U^{\frac{1}{2}} - 2v^{\frac{1}{2}} \Rightarrow kx = 2U^{\frac{3}{2}}(U^{\frac{1}{2}} - v^{\frac{1}{2}})$$

and $\displaystyle x = \frac{2U^{\frac{3}{2}}}{k}(U^{\frac{1}{2}} - v^{\frac{1}{2}}) \qquad \qquad \dots ⑤$

The **maximum distance** away from the origin is when the **velocity is zero**.

Putting $v = 0$ into ⑤ gives $x = \dfrac{2U^2}{k}$

For the second part we need the other form for the acceleration, $\dfrac{dv}{dt}$.

Putting this in for a in equation ②,

$$\frac{dv}{dt} = -k\left(\frac{v}{U}\right)^{\frac{3}{2}} \quad \text{and rearranging}$$

$$\int \frac{dv}{v^{\frac{3}{2}}} = \frac{-k}{U^{\frac{3}{2}}}\int dt \quad \Rightarrow \quad -\frac{2}{v^{\frac{1}{2}}} = \frac{-kt}{U^{\frac{3}{2}}} + C \qquad \dots ⑥$$

We're told that $v = U$ when $t = 0$, so

$$-\frac{2}{u^{\frac{1}{2}}} = C \quad \text{and} \ \textcircled{6} \text{ becomes} \quad -\frac{2}{v^{\frac{1}{2}}} = \frac{-kt}{u^{\frac{3}{2}}} - \frac{2}{u^{\frac{1}{2}}}$$

$$\Rightarrow \frac{2}{\sqrt{v}} = \frac{1}{\sqrt{u}}\left[\frac{kt}{u} + 2\right] = \frac{1}{\sqrt{u}}\left[\frac{kt + 2u}{u}\right]$$

$$\Rightarrow \frac{\sqrt{v}}{2} = \sqrt{u}\left[\frac{u}{kt + 2u}\right]$$

$$\Rightarrow v = 4u\left[\frac{u}{kt + 2u}\right]^2$$

Proportional forces

In the previous example the expression for the force included the positive constant k. Instead of being given an expression for the force, we can be told that it is **proportional to** some variable term, like v^2 or the square root of the distance. Then we have to rewrite this information in the form of an equation, i.e. $F = kv^2$ or $F = k\sqrt{x}$, and state that k is a positive constant.

Example	A particle is projected from O with velocity u (where $u > 0$) and moves under the action of a force directed towards O and proportional to $v^{\frac{3}{2}}$ When $x = a$ the velocity of the particle is $\frac{u}{4}$. Find the velocity when $x = \frac{4a}{3}$.

Solution	The two points to note about the force are that it is directed towards O, i.e. against the direction of motion, and so is negative, and that it is **proportional to** $v^{\frac{3}{2}}$. Combining these two points in one equation,

$$F = -kv^{\frac{3}{2}} \quad \text{where } k \text{ is a positive constant.}$$

We're not given a mass in this case – putting $F = ma$ in the above equation gives

$$ma = -kv^{\frac{3}{2}} \Rightarrow a = \frac{-k}{m}v^{\frac{3}{2}} \qquad \dots \textcircled{1}$$

We want an expression combining distance and velocity, and so we use $a = v\dfrac{dv}{dx}$ and $\textcircled{1}$ becomes

$$v\frac{dv}{dx} = \frac{-k}{m}v^{\frac{3}{2}} \qquad \dots \textcircled{2}$$

and rearranging,

$$\int \frac{v\,dv}{v^{\frac{3}{2}}} = \int -\frac{k}{m}\,dx \quad \text{or} \quad \int \frac{dv}{v^{\frac{1}{2}}} = \frac{-k}{m}\int dx \qquad \dots ③$$

$$\Rightarrow \quad 2v^{\frac{1}{2}} = \frac{-k}{m}x + C \qquad \dots ④$$

We have **two** constants here and so we need two sets of limits to eliminate them. We're told that $v = u$ when $x = 0$

$$\Rightarrow \quad 2u^{\frac{1}{2}} = C \quad \text{and} \; ④ \; \text{becomes}$$

$$2v^{\frac{1}{2}} = \frac{-k}{m}x + 2u^{\frac{1}{2}} \qquad \dots ⑤$$

Also we're told that when $x = a$, $v = \dfrac{u}{4}$

$$2\left(\frac{u}{4}\right)^{\frac{1}{2}} = \frac{-k}{m}a + 2u^{\frac{1}{2}}$$

$$\Rightarrow \quad 2 \times \frac{u^{\frac{1}{2}}}{2} = \frac{-k}{m}a + 2u^{\frac{1}{2}}$$

$$\Rightarrow \quad \frac{k}{m}a = u^{\frac{1}{2}} \quad \Rightarrow \quad \frac{k}{m} = \frac{u^{\frac{1}{2}}}{a}$$

Putting this into ⑤,

$$2v^{\frac{1}{2}} = -\left(\frac{u^{\frac{1}{2}}}{a}\right)x + 2u^{\frac{1}{2}} \qquad \dots ⑥$$

and so when $x = \dfrac{4a}{3}$

$$2v^{\frac{1}{2}} = -\frac{u^{\frac{1}{2}}}{a} \times \frac{4a}{3} + 2u^{\frac{1}{2}} = \frac{2u^{\frac{1}{2}}}{3}$$

$$\Rightarrow \quad v^{\frac{1}{2}} = \frac{u^{\frac{1}{2}}}{3} \quad \text{and} \; v = \frac{u}{9} \; \text{by squaring.}$$

Discontinuous forces and accelerations

The force acting on a particle can change abruptly at some point – in this case there will be two (or more) expressions for the force which apply only in the appropriate interval. Here's an example of this kind.

Example

A particle P of unit mass moves on the positive x-axis. At time t the velocity of the particle is v, and the force F acting on P in the positive direction is given by:

$$F = \frac{50}{25 + v} \quad \text{for } 0 \le t \le 50,$$

and $\quad F = -\dfrac{v^2}{1000} \quad$ for $t > 50$.

Initially the particle is at rest at the origin O. Show that $v = 50$ when $t = 50$.

Find:

(a) the distance of P from O when $v = 50$

(b) the distance of P from O when $v = 25$ and $t > 50$.

Solution

We're told that the particle has **unit mass**, i.e. $m = 1$ and so the expression for the force is the same as that for the acceleration. We want an expression for v in terms of t, and so we use $\dfrac{dv}{dt}$ for the acceleration, and since we'll be using $t = 50$, the first force is the appropriate one, since the second only comes into operation when $t > 50$.

$$\frac{dv}{dt} = \frac{50}{25 + v}$$

$$\int (25 + v)dv = \int 50dt$$

$$25v + \frac{v^2}{2} = 50t + C$$

Initially, i.e. $t = 0$, the particle is at rest, i.e. $v = 0$. Substituting this pair of values, $C = 0$ and so

$$25v + \frac{v^2}{2} = 50t \qquad \qquad \text{... ①}$$

We want to find the value of v when $t = 50$

$$25v + \frac{v^2}{2} = 50 \times 50 = 2500 \qquad \times 2 \text{ and rearrange}$$

$$v^2 + 50v - 5000 = 0$$

$$(v - 50)(v + 100) = 0$$

Since the acceleration is **positive** up to $t = 50$, the velocity cannot be negative, and so $v = 50$.

(a) We now want distances, so we use $a = v\dfrac{dv}{dx}$ in the first expression for the force:

$$v\frac{dv}{dx} = \frac{50}{25 + v} \;\Rightarrow\; \int v(25 + v)dv = \int 50dx$$

$$\Rightarrow \int (25v + v^2)dv = 50x + C$$

$$\Rightarrow \frac{25v^2}{2} + \frac{v^3}{3} = 50x + D$$

But when $x = 0$, $v = 0 \Rightarrow D = 0$ and

$$\frac{25v^2}{2} + \frac{v^3}{3} = 50x$$

When $v = 50$, $x = \dfrac{1}{50}\left(\dfrac{25v^2}{2} + \dfrac{v^3}{3}\right) = \dfrac{25 \times 50}{2} + \dfrac{50^2}{3} = 1458\tfrac{1}{3}$

(b) When $t > 50$, the second expression for the force applies, and so

$$a = \frac{-v^2}{1000}$$

and since distance is involved

$$v\frac{dv}{dx} = \frac{-v^2}{1000} \;\Rightarrow\; \int v\frac{dv}{v^2} = \int \frac{-dx}{1000}$$

$$\Rightarrow \int \frac{dv}{v} = -\frac{1}{1000}x + C$$

$$\Rightarrow \ln v = -\frac{x}{1000} + C \qquad\qquad \text{... ①}$$

Now $v = 50$ when $t = 50$ and at this point, $x = 1458\tfrac{1}{3}$, from (a).

Putting these values in,

$$\ln 50 = -\frac{1458\tfrac{1}{3}}{1000} + C$$

$$\Rightarrow C = \ln 50 + \frac{1458\tfrac{1}{3}}{1000} = \ln 50 + \frac{35}{24}$$

① then becomes $\ln v = \dfrac{-x}{1000} + \ln 50 + \dfrac{35}{24}$

and when $v = 25$, $\dfrac{x}{1000} = \ln 50 + \dfrac{35}{24} - \ln 25 = \ln 2 + \dfrac{35}{24}$

$$\Rightarrow x = 2151.5 \text{ (1 d.p.)}$$

You should now be able to answer Exercises 6–11 on pp. 15–17.

Gravity

When a particle is moving vertically, it will have a gravitational force acting in addition to any other force. Here's an example of this.

Example

A particle P of mass m moves in a medium which produces a resistance of magnitude mkv, where v is the speed of P and k is a constant. The particle P is projected vertically upwards in this medium with speed $\frac{g}{k}$. Show that P comes momentarily to rest after time $\frac{\ln 2}{k}$.

Solution

Both forces acting on the particle are slowing it down (when $v > 0$).

Figure 1.2

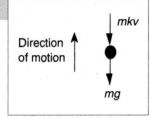

$$F = ma = -[mg + mkv] = -m[g + kv]$$

Putting $a = \dfrac{dv}{dt}$ gives

$$m\frac{dv}{dt} = -m[g + kv]$$

$$\Rightarrow \int \frac{dv}{g + kv} = -\int dt$$

$$\frac{1}{k}\ln(g + kv) = -t + C$$

$$t = 0, v = \frac{g}{k} \Rightarrow \frac{1}{k}\ln(g + g) = C = \frac{1}{k}\ln 2g$$

i.e. $\dfrac{1}{k}\ln(g + kv) = -t + \dfrac{1}{k}\ln 2g$

when $v = 0$, $\dfrac{1}{k}\ln g = -t + \dfrac{1}{k}\ln 2g$

$$\Rightarrow t = \frac{1}{k}(\ln 2g - \ln g) = \frac{1}{k}\ln\frac{2g}{g} = \frac{1}{k}\ln 2$$

You should now be able to answer Exercise 12 on p. 17.

EXERCISES

1 Find: (a) $\displaystyle\int \frac{v}{v^2 + 3v + 2}\, dv$ (b) $\displaystyle\int \frac{v}{v-2}\, dv$ (c) $\displaystyle\int \frac{v}{1 - 3v^2}\, dv$

2 A particle P moves along the x-axis with acceleration $6e^{-3t}$ at time t. Its velocity at time t is denoted by v, when $t = 0$, $v = 1$. Find the value of t when $v = 2$. Find also the limiting value of the speed as t becomes large.

3 A particle moves along a straight line with acceleration $\dfrac{k}{v}$, where k is a constant and v is the velocity of the particle. When the particle is at a point O its velocity is 1 m s^{-1}, and when its displacement from O is 13 metres its velocity is 3 m s^{-1}. Show that $k = \frac{2}{3}$. Find the velocity of the particle when it is at the point A whose displacement from O is 62 metres.

Find also the time taken for the particle to travel from O to A.

4 A particle moves along Ox in the positive direction. At time $t = 0$, its speed is 8 m s^{-1}. At time t s, its acceleration is $3e^{2t}$ m s^{-2} in the positive direction. Calculate, in metres to 3 significant figures, the distance the particle moves in the first 2 seconds.

5 A particle of mass m is travelling in a horizontal straight line with velocity u. It is brought to rest by means of a resisting force of magnitude $km(2u - v)$, where v is the velocity of the particle at any instant and k is a positive constant. Show that the distance travelled while v decreases from u to zero is $\dfrac{u(\ln 4 - 1)}{k}$.

6 A particle Q, of mass m, moves along the x-axis in the positive direction and at time t it has velocity v. At time $t = 0$, it is at the origin and $v = U$. The only force acting on the particle opposes the motion of the particle and is of magnitude $k\sqrt{v}$ where k is a constant. Find v in terms of m, U, k and t only, and show that the particle comes to rest at a distance $\dfrac{2mU^{\frac{3}{2}}}{3k}$ from the origin.

7 A particle of mass m is projected upwards from a point P on the earth's surface. It experiences a force, of magnitude $\dfrac{(mgR^2)}{x^2}$, directed towards the centre O of the earth, where R is the radius of the earth and x is the distance of the particle from O. Given that the particle is projected with speed $\sqrt{gR}$ in the direction OP, find how far it will have travelled when its speed is $\frac{1}{2}\sqrt{gR}$.

8 A particle moves on the positive x-axis. The particle is moving towards the origin O when it passes through the point A, where $x = 2a$, with speed $\sqrt{\dfrac{k}{a}}$, where k is constant. Given that the particle experiences an acceleration $\dfrac{k}{2x^2} + \dfrac{k}{4a^2}$ in a direction away from O, show that it comes instantaneously to rest at a point B, where $x = a$. Immediately the particle reaches B the acceleration changes to $\dfrac{k}{2x^2} - \dfrac{k}{4a^2}$ in a direction away from O. Show that the particle next comes instantaneously to rest at A.

(Be careful with the signs in this one.)

9 A particle P moves on the x-axis under the action of a force of variable magnitude directed along the axis. At time t seconds the displacement of P from the origin O is x metres, and the velocity and acceleration of P, both in the positive x-direction, are $v\,\mathrm{m\,s^{-1}}$ and $a\,\mathrm{m\,s^{-2}}$ respectively.

(a) Given that $a = 6x - 4x^3$ and that, when $x = 1$, $v = 0$, show that v is also zero when $x = \sqrt{2}$.

(b) Given that $a = -v^4$ and that, when $t = 0$, $x = 0$ and $v = 2$, find x and t in terms of v. Show that the average speed $\Big($remember that average speed $= \dfrac{\text{total distance}}{\text{total time}}\Big)$ over the time interval in which v decreases from 2 to 1 is $\dfrac{9}{7}\,\mathrm{m\,s^{-1}}$.

10 A particle of mass 0.5 kg, moves in a horizontal straight line, starting from a point O with a speed of 24 $\mathrm{m\,s^{-1}}$. When the particle has travelled a distance s m, in time t s, its speed is v m $\mathrm{s^{-1}}$ and its acceleration is a m $\mathrm{s^{-2}}$, where

$$a = -0.2v.$$

(a) Obtain an expression for v in terms of t.

(b) Obtain, in terms of t, an expression for the force acting on the particle at time t.

(c) Determine the relationship which exists between v and s.

(d) When the particle reaches the point P its speed has been reduced to 12 $\mathrm{m\,s^{-1}}$. Calculate:

(i) the distance OP

(ii) the time taken to travel from O to P.

11 A particle moves in a straight line from a point O with initial speed u. At time t, where $t \geq 0$, after leaving O, the acceleration of the particle is $\dfrac{\lambda}{v}$, where v is the speed of the particle and λ is a positive constant.

At the instant when $t = T$, the particle is at the point A and is moving with speed $2u$.

(a) By forming and solving a differential equation in v and t, show that
$$2\lambda T = 3u^2.$$

(b) Show that the distance between O and A is $\dfrac{7u^3}{3\lambda}$.

(c) Find, in terms of u, the speed of the particle at the point B, where $OB = 2OA$.

12 A particle of mass 1 kg falls vertically through a liquid. The motion of the particle is resisted by a force of magnitude $2v$ newtons, where $v\,\mathrm{ms}^{-1}$ is the speed of the particle at time t seconds. Show that:
$$\left(\frac{1}{5-v}\right)\frac{dv}{dt} = 2$$

and hence find, correct to 3 significant figures, the value of v when $t = 1$, given that $v = 0$ when $t = 0$.

SUMMARY

Having completed this section on variable acceleration, you should now be able to:

- recognise the types of problems which involve variable acceleration, including those with variable force
- distinguish between an acceleration and a retardation, or the forces producing these, and attach an appropriate sign
- set up and solve the appropriate differential equation to produce the required solution
- know when and how to use the two main forms for acceleration
$$\frac{dv}{dt} \quad \text{and} \quad v\frac{dv}{dx}$$
- translate the information given in the question into mathematical terms so that constants can be evaluated
- appreciate that maximum distance means the velocity is zero, maximum velocity means the acceleration is zero.

Momentum and impulse

When two objects collide, we have seen from our work on this topic in Module M1 that momentum is conserved: applying this principle gives us one equation connecting the velocities before and after the collision. In order to solve more general systems we need a further equation. This comes from applying Newton's Experimental Law, which states that in a collision between two objects

$$\frac{\text{speed of separation}}{\text{speed of approach}} = e$$

where e is a constant for any two bodies called the **coefficient of restitution**. Most of the work in this section will deal with solving problems by finding equations coming from these two sources.

For your work on this section you will need to be familiar with:

● simultaneous equations

● the work on momentum in M1 (Section 7).

Coefficient of restitution (e)

This measures the elasticity of the two bodies and takes a value between 0 and 1. If $e = 0$, the bodies are said to be **perfectly inelastic** and if $e = 1$, the bodies are said to be **perfectly elastic**.

One of the simplest examples of this is a moving particle colliding with a fixed surface with velocity u, where the coefficient of restitution between the particle and surface is e. If the velocity with which the particle rebounds is v, then by Newton's Experimental Law,

$$\frac{\text{Speed of separation (i.e. relative speed)}}{\text{Speed of approach (i.e. relative speed)}} = \frac{v}{u} = e$$

$$\text{i.e. } v = eu$$

Here's an example of this.

| Example | A sphere of mass m is dropped from a height of h on to a horizontal floor. Find the height to which the sphere rebounds if the coefficient of restitution between sphere and floor is $\frac{1}{2}$. |

| Solution | We can find the velocity of the sphere immediately before the collision by equating the loss in potential energy with the gain in kinetic energy. |

Figure 2.1

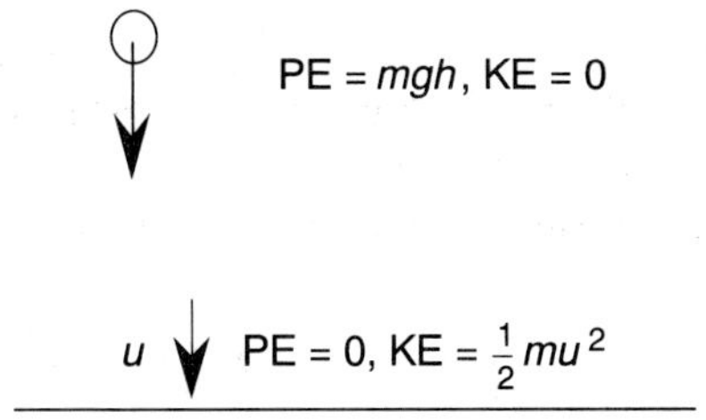

i.e. $\frac{1}{2}mu^2 = mgh \implies u^2 = 2gh$

$u = \sqrt{2gh}$

The velocity v after the collision is given by eu,

i.e. $e\sqrt{2gh}$ or $\frac{1}{2}\sqrt{2gh}$, since $e = \frac{1}{2}$

This gives the new kinetic energy as

$$\frac{1}{2}mv^2 = \frac{1}{2}m \times \left[\frac{1}{2}\sqrt{2gh}\right]^2 = \frac{1}{2}m \times \frac{1}{4}2gh = \frac{mgh}{4}$$

For maximum height, this kinetic energy will all be converted into potential energy. If the height is H, the potential energy will be mgH and so:

$$mgH = mg\frac{h}{4} \implies H = \frac{h}{4}$$

i.e. the sphere will rebound to one quarter of its original height.

Here is an example of a more practical situation where we model cars by particles and apply our equations to these.

Example
A queue of cars is stationary when the last one is hit in the rear by another car. The situation is modelled by a series of stationary particles each of mass 1500 kg lying in a straight line, the last one of which is struck by another particle of the same mass travelling with a speed of 40 km per hour along the line of stationary particles. The coefficient of restitution between any of the particles is e and it is assumed that the particles move with constant velocity between impacts.

Find the speed of the car which was originally next to last in the queue after it has been struck by the one behind.

Modern cars tend to be designed with 'crumple zones' at the front and rear which collapse on impact from these directions and help to absorb the energy of a collision. Determine, with reasons, whether such 'crumple zones' are modelled by a high or low value of e.

Solution
We draw a sketch and put in the usual information.

Figure 2.2

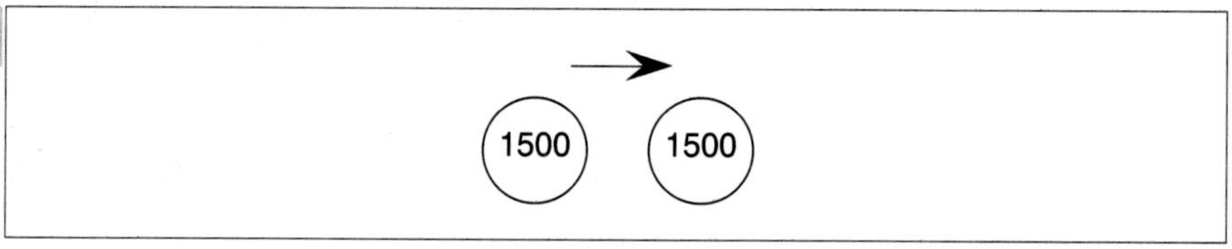

Velocity before	40	0
Velocity after	v_1	v_2

By momentum: $1500 \times 40 = 1500v_1 + 1500v_2$

i.e. $40 = v_1 + v_2$ ... ①

By restitution: $\dfrac{v_2 - v_1}{40} = e$

$\Rightarrow 40e = v_2 - v_1$ ... ②

Adding these: $40(1 + e) = 2v_2 \Rightarrow v_2 = 20(1 + e)$

For the second collision, the equations are the same, except that 40 is replaced by $20(1 + e)$

$\Rightarrow \quad 20(1 + e) = v_3 + v_4$ ... ③

$20e(1 + e) = v_4 - v_3$ ... ④

where v_3 and v_4 are the velocities of the last and next-to-last cars in the queue respectively, after their collision.

This gives: $2v_4 = 20(1 + e)^2$

$\Rightarrow \quad v_4 = 10(1 + e)^2$

You can see from the last equation that the higher the value for e, the greater the speed of the car after collision. In fact, if $e = 1$, the speed after collision is the same as the speed of the colliding car – this is a perfectly elastic collision where no energy is lost. This is the reverse of what the designer requires. With a low value for e, the speed after collision of the car that is hit is only half that of the colliding car, and most of the energy has been absorbed by the crumple zones.

Let's have a look at another example where we use Newton's Experimental Law to find the loss of kinetic energy in a collision.

Example

Two small spheres A and B, having masses $4m$ and $5m$ respectively, move directly towards each other and collide. Immediately before the collision the speeds of A and B are $5u$ and $4u$ respectively. Given that the coefficient of restitution is $\frac{1}{3}$, find the loss of kinetic energy in the collision.

Solution

For the positive direction, we can take A's original direction of motion

Figure 2.3

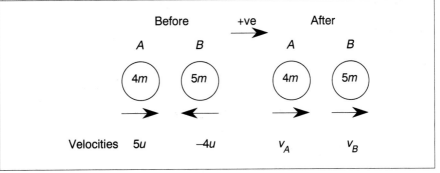

(Note that B's velocity before is **negative** since it's moving **towards** A.)

Conservation of momentum: $(4m)(5u) + (5m)(-4u) = 4mv_A + 5mv_B$ ... ①

(Note that we've assumed that the particles will be moving in a **positive** direction after the collision – if in fact one or both are moving in the opposite direction, their velocities will turn out to be negative when we solve the equations.)

Newton's Experimental Law: $\dfrac{\text{Separation speed}}{\text{Approach speed}} = \dfrac{1}{3} \Rightarrow \dfrac{v_B - v_A}{5u - (-4u)} = \dfrac{1}{3}$ ... ②

We'll now simplify equations ① and ②:

① becomes $20mu - 20mu = 4mv_A + 5mv_B$

$0 = 4mv_A + 5mv_B$

Dividing by m and swapping sides,

$4v_A + 5v_B = 0$ ... ①'

② becomes $\dfrac{v_B - v_A}{5u + 4u} = \dfrac{1}{3} \implies \dfrac{v_B - v_A}{9u} = \dfrac{1}{3}$

$$v_B - v_A = \frac{9u}{3} = 3u \qquad \text{... ②}$$

Solving ① and ② simultaneously, we want the coefficients of either v_A or v_B to be the same, so we can multiply ② by 4 and then have:

$$4v_A + 5v_B = 0 \qquad \text{... ①''}$$

$$4v_B - 4v_A = 12u \qquad \text{... ②''}$$

Adding these, $9v_B = 12u$

$$\implies v_B = \frac{12u}{9} = \frac{4u}{3} \qquad \text{... ③}$$

Putting this into ①: $4v_A + 5\left(\dfrac{4u}{3}\right) = 0$

$$4v_A + \frac{20u}{3} = 0 \implies 4v_A = \frac{-20u}{3}$$

$$\implies v_A = \frac{-5u}{3} \qquad \text{... ④}$$

So the velocity of each sphere afterwards has the opposite sign to the velocity before, i.e. they both rebound after the collision.

The kinetic energy is given by $\frac{1}{2}$ mass $\times$ velocity^2 for each particle.

Total kinetic energy before is $\frac{1}{2}(4m)(5u)^2 + \frac{1}{2}(5m)(-4u)^2$

$$= \frac{1}{2} \times 4m \times 25u^2 + \frac{1}{2} \times 5m \times 16u^2$$

$$= 50mu^2 + 40mu^2 = 90mu^2$$

KE after is $\frac{1}{2}(4m)(-\dfrac{5u}{3})^2 + \frac{1}{2}(5m)(\dfrac{4u}{3})^2$

$$= \frac{1}{2} \times 4m \times \frac{25u^2}{9} + \frac{1}{2} \times 5m \times \frac{16u^2}{9}$$

$$= \frac{50u^2}{9} + \frac{40mu^2}{9} = \frac{90mu^2}{9} = 10mu^2$$

So the loss of kinetic energy is $90mu^2 - 10mu^2 = 80mu^2$

There will always be a loss of kinetic energy in a simple collision between two particles unless the collision is **perfectly elastic**, i.e. $e = 1$.

You should now be able to answer Exercises 1–3 on pp. 25–26.

Here is a further example involving more than one collision.

Example

Three particles A, B and C have masses m, $3m$ and λm respectively. The particles lie at rest on a smooth horizontal plane in a straight line with B between A and C. Particle A is given a horizontal impulse, of magnitude J, and collides directly with B. After this collision A is at rest and B moves towards C with speed u. The coefficient of restitution at each impact is e.

(a) Find J in terms of m and u.

(b) Show that $e = \dfrac{1}{3}$.

(c) Find, in terms of m and u, the loss in kinetic energy in the collision between A and B.

Particle B, moving with speed u, collides directly with particle C.

(d) Find, in terms of λ and u, the speeds of B and C after their collision.

(e) Show that A and B will have a second collision provided that $\lambda > 9$.

(f) Given that $\lambda = 6$, find, in terms of m and u, the magnitude of the impulse on B in the collision between B and C.

Solution

(a) For the initial impulse,

Figure 2.4

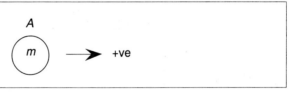

	Velocity before	0	Momentum before	0
	Velocity after	v_A	Momentum after	mv_A

Change in momentum is $mv_A - 0 = mv_A$. Since this is the impulse,

$$J = mv_A \qquad \qquad \dots \text{①}$$

$$v_A = \frac{J}{m}$$

Figure 2.5

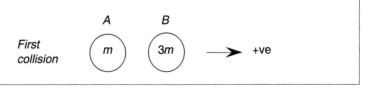

First collision

		A	B
Velocity before		$\dfrac{J}{m}$	0
Velocity after		0	u
Momentum before		J	0
Momentum after		0	$3mu$

By conservation of momentum,

$$J + 0 = 0 + 3mu \implies J = 3mu \qquad \dots ②$$

(b) Relative speed before is $\dfrac{J}{m}$

Relative speed after is u

By law of restitution, $\dfrac{u}{\dfrac{J}{m}} = e \implies Je = mu \implies J = \dfrac{mu}{e} \qquad \dots ③$

Putting ② and ③ together

$$3mu = \dfrac{mu}{e} \implies e = \dfrac{1}{3}$$

(c) Putting ① and ② together

$$mv_A = 3mu$$

so $\quad v_A = 3u$

KE before is $\dfrac{1}{2} \times m \times (3u)^2 + 0$

KE after is $0 + \dfrac{1}{2} \times 3m \times u^2$

Loss in KE = KE before − KE after $= \dfrac{9mu^2}{2} - \dfrac{3mu^2}{2} = \dfrac{6mu^2}{2} = 3mu^2$

(d)

Figure 2.6

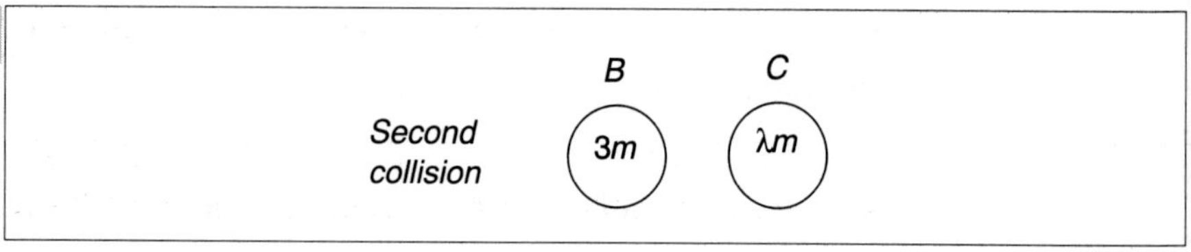

	B	C
Second collision	$3m$	λm
Velocity before	u	0
Velocity after	v_B	v_C

Momentum : $3mu = 3mv_B + \lambda m v_C$

i.e. $3v_B + \lambda v_C = 3u \qquad \dots ④$

Restitution : $\dfrac{v_C - v_B}{u} = e = \dfrac{1}{3}$ (answer to part (b))

i.e. $\quad v_C - v_B = \dfrac{u}{3} \qquad \dots ⑤$

⑤ × 3 $\qquad 3v_C - 3v_B = u \qquad \dots ⑥$

④ + ⑥ $\qquad 3v_C + \lambda v_C = 4u$

$\qquad\qquad (3 + \lambda)v_C = 4u$

$$v_C = \dfrac{4u}{3 + \lambda}$$

This into ⑤ $\dfrac{4u}{3+\lambda} - v_B = \dfrac{u}{3}$

$$v_B = \dfrac{4u}{3+\lambda} - \dfrac{u}{3} = \dfrac{12u - 3u - \lambda u}{3(3+\lambda)} = \dfrac{u(9-\lambda)}{3(3+\lambda)}$$

(e) Since after the first collision between A and B, A is brought to rest, there will be a second collision provided that B's velocity is towards A after B's collision with C, i.e. provided that $v_B < 0$

i.e. $\dfrac{u(9-\lambda)}{3(3+\lambda)} < 0$

We can multiply through by $3(3+\lambda)$, since this is positive

$$u(9-\lambda) < 0$$

and divide through by u, since this is also positive

$$9 - \lambda < 0 \implies \lambda > 9$$

(f) If $\lambda = 6$, $v_C = \dfrac{4u}{9}$ and the momentum of C after the collision with B is

mass × velocity

$$\lambda m \times \dfrac{4u}{9} \implies 6m \times \dfrac{4u}{9} = \dfrac{8u}{3}$$

This is the **impulse** of B on C since C was originally at rest, with zero momentum, and impulse is change in momentum. So the impulse of C on B is $\dfrac{-8u}{3}$ (always equal and opposite) with magnitude $\dfrac{8u}{3}$ (ignoring the minus sign).

You should now be able to answer Exercises 4–9 on pp. 26–28.

EXERCISES

1 Two smooth spheres A and B of equal radii and masses $3m$ and m, respectively, are travelling towards each other along the line of centres. Given that each has speed u and that the collision is perfectly elastic:

(a) show that A is brought to rest by the impact

(b) find the speed of B after the impact.

2 Two spheres A and B, of mass $3m$ and m respectively, are moving towards each other with speeds of $4u$ and u respectively. Find the velocity of each sphere after the collision and show that the loss in kinetic energy is $9mu^2$, given that the coefficient of restitution between the two spheres is $\dfrac{1}{5}$.

3 Two particles, A and B, of masses $2m$ and $3m$ respectively, are moving in a straight line in the same direction on a smooth horizontal plane. The particles collide and, *after* the collision, A and B continue to move in the same straight line and in the same direction with speeds u and $\frac{3u}{2}$ respectively. Given that the coefficient of restitution between A and B is $\frac{1}{5}$, find, in terms of u, the speed of A and the speed of B *before* their collision. Find also, in terms of m and u, the magnitude of the impulse of the force exerted by B on A during the collision.

4 Three small smooth spheres A, B and C, of masses $15m$, $5m$ and λm, are at rest in a straight line on a horizontal plane. Sphere A then moves along the plane and strikes directly sphere B which moves off with speed v. Sphere B goes on to strike sphere C directly. The coefficient of restitution between each pair of spheres is $\frac{1}{2}$.

(a) Find, in terms of v, the speed of A before and after impact with B.

(b) Find, in terms of m and v the change in:

    (i) the magnitude of the momentum of A

    (ii) the magnitude of the momentum of B, as a result of their collision.

Given that, after the impact of B with C, there are no further collisions, show that $\lambda \leq \frac{40}{19}$.

5 Two small smooth spheres P and Q of equal radii but of masses m and $3m$ respectively are moving towards each other on a smooth horizontal table. Before collision the speeds of P and Q are $3u$ and $6u$ respectively and after collision the direction of motion of P is reversed and it moves with speed $5u$. Find the impulse on Q, the speed of Q after the collision and the coefficient of restitution between P and Q.

After collision, P moves with constant speed $5u$ until it catches up, and collides directly, with a third sphere S which is identical to P and which is moving in the same direction with speed $2u$. The kinetic energy lost in this second collision is $2mu^2$. Find the speed of P immediately after colliding with S. (The coefficient of restitution between P and S is not the same as that between P and Q.)

6 A uniform smooth sphere A, of mass m, lies on a smooth horizontal table between a second uniform smooth sphere B, of equal size but of mass λm ($\lambda > 0$), and a fixed vertical plane. The line joining the centres of the spheres is normal to the plane. Between both the spheres and between a sphere and the plane the coefficient of restitution is $\frac{3}{5}$.

Sphere A is projected along the table with speed u towaards sphere B. Show that the direction of motion of A is reversed in the collision provided that $\lambda > \frac{5}{3}$. Also show that in this case sphere A, after rebounding from the vertical plane, will collide again with sphere B provided that $\lambda > \frac{55}{9}$.

Given that $\lambda = 15$ show that sphere A is reduced to rest after its second collision with B and find the final velocity of B.

7 The coefficient of restitution between two particles A and B is e, where $0 < e < 1$. The masses of A and B are m and em respectively. The particles are moving with constant speeds u and eu in the same horizontal line, and in the same direction, and they collide.

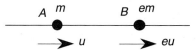

(a) Show that after the collision the speed of A is $u(1 - e + e^2)$ and that the speed of B is independent of e.

(b) Find the value of e for which the speed of A after the collision is least and deduce that, in this case, the total loss of kinetic energy due to the collision is $\frac{1}{32} mu^2$.

(c) Find the possible values of e for which the impulse of the force exerted by B on A due to the collision has magnitude $\frac{6}{25} mu$.

8 Two small spheres P and Q, of equal radii and having masses $4m$ and m respectively, are placed at rest on a smooth horizontal plane. The line PQ is perpendicular to a fixed vertical barrier with Q between P and the barrier. The coefficient of restitution between Q and the barrier is $\frac{1}{2}$ and between P and Q is $\frac{2}{3}$.

The sphere Q is projected, with speed U, directly towards the barrier. Show that the kinetic energy lost when Q collides with the barrier is $\frac{3}{8} mU^2$.

Determine how many collisions take place altogether and, for the second collision, find the loss of kinetic energy of the system and find the magnitude of the impulse on Q.

9 A ball is thrown vertically upwards with speed U from a point halfway between the floor and ceiling of a room of height h. After rebounding from the ceiling and then the floor it just reaches the ceiling a second time. The coefficient of restitution at both floor and ceiling is $\frac{1}{2}$. Denoting the speed of the ball just before its first impact with the floor by V, show that

$$V = \sqrt{(8gh)}$$

and find U in terms of g and h.

Find the ratio of the magnitude of the impulse when the ball first reaches the ceiling to the magnitude of the impulse on the floor.

SUMMARY

This section has covered the relationship between momentum and impulse, and explored the mathematical background to collisions between objects. You should now:

- be able to set up a pair of simultaneous equations using conservation of momentum and Newton's Experimental law.
- be able to solve these equations to find the unknowns
- know that $0 < e < 1$ and use this fact to derive given inequalities
- know the conditions necessary for further collisions when three particles are involved.

3

Elastic strings

In this section we shall be looking firstly at static systems, where the elastic string(s) and masses are in equilibrium. We shall then move on to systems where the particle is moving, and use the principle of conservation of mechanical energy where, in addition to the kinetic and gravitational potential energies, we now have elastic potential energy.

Before you start your work on this section, you may find it helpful to look over the work on conservation of energy in Module M1.

Hooke's Law

The fundamental law that applies in work on elastic strings is called **Hooke's Law** and states that the tension is directly proportional to the extension in the string.

Hooke's Law

$$T = \frac{\lambda x}{l}$$

where x is the extension, *l* the natural length of the elastic string
and λ is a constant for any particular string
called the **modulus of elasticity**.

The equation $T = \dfrac{\lambda x}{l}$ enables us to find what **mass** suspended on one end of the string will cause a given **extension** and vice versa. Since the tension is directly proportional to the extension, twice the mass will produce twice the extension. Here are some examples which use the basic equation.

Example	An elastic string of natural length 2 m has a modulus of elasticity of $3g$ N. Find the extension when a particle of mass 4 kg is suspended from one end.

Solution	Look at Figure 3.1.

Figure 3.1	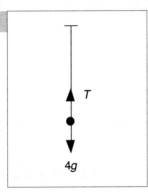	Since the system is in equilibrium,

$$T - 4g = 0 \implies T = 4g$$

But since $T = \dfrac{\lambda x}{l}$ and $\lambda = 3g, l = 2$

$$4g = \frac{3gx}{2} \implies x = \frac{8}{3}$$

Example	A mass of 4 kg suspended on one end of an elastic string produces an extension of 2 m. Find the modulus of elasticity if the natural length is 5 m.

Solution	$T = 4g$ and also $T = \dfrac{\lambda x}{l}$.

Since $x = 2$, and $l = 5$ (given), $4g = \dfrac{\lambda \times 2}{5}$

$$\implies \lambda = 10g, \text{ i.e. the modulus is } 10g \text{ N}$$

(Note that the units of the modulus are those of a force, i.e. Newtons)

You should now be able to answer Exercises 1–2 on p. 42.

Let's have a look now at some questions involving slightly more complicated systems. Here's one where an elastic string passes over a smooth peg.

Example	A light elastic string, of natural length l and modulus of elasticity $4mg$, has one end tied to a fixed point A. The string passes over a fixed smooth peg B and at the other end a particle P, of mass m, is attached. The particle hangs in equilibrium. The distance between A and B is l and AB is inclined at 60° to the vertical as shown in Figure 3.2.

Figure 3.2

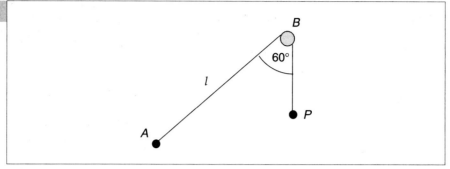

(a) Find, in terms of l, the length of the vertical portion BP of the string.

(b) Show that the magnitude of the force exerted by the string on the peg is $mg\sqrt{3}$.

Solution   (a) Since the peg is smooth, the tension will be the same on either side:

Figure 3.3

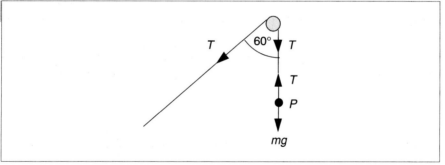

The system is in equilibrium, so the net force acting on the particle P must be zero, i.e.

$$T - mg = 0 \qquad \qquad \dots ①$$

But since the string is elastic, natural length l and $\lambda = 4mg$,

$$T = \frac{\lambda x}{l} = \frac{4mg\,x}{l} \qquad \qquad \dots ②$$

Substituting this into ①, $\dfrac{4mg\,x}{l} - mg = 0$

$$mg\left(\frac{4x}{l} - 1\right) = 0 \quad \Rightarrow \quad \frac{4x}{l} - 1 = 0 \quad \text{since } mg \neq 0$$

$$\Rightarrow x = \frac{l}{4}$$

Since AB is l, the natural length, this extension of $\dfrac{l}{4}$ is the required length BP.

(b) The force exerted by the string on the peg will be the resultant of the two equal tensions in each part of the string.

Figure 3.4

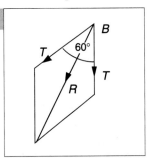

Resolving along the bisector of the angle at B,

$$R = 2T \cos 30° = 2T \times \frac{\sqrt{3}}{2} = T\sqrt{3}$$

But from ①, $T = mg \Rightarrow$ magnitude of the resultant is $mg\sqrt{3}$ as required.

We will now look at another example, this time involving **two** connected elastic strings.

Example

Two light elastic strings AB and CD each have natural length l and an extension of $\frac{l}{2}$ is produced in each string by tensions mg and $2mg$ respectively. The strings are joined at their ends B and C and the end A is fastened to a fixed point. From the end D is hung a particle of mass m. Show that, when the mass m hangs at rest vertically below A, the total extension in the combined string $ABCD$ is $\frac{3l}{4}$.

Solution

We'll calculate the moduli of elasticity of each string first of all.

$$AB: \quad T_1 = \frac{\lambda_1 x}{l} \Rightarrow mg = \frac{\frac{\lambda_1 l}{2}}{l} \Rightarrow \lambda_1 = 2mg \qquad \dots ①$$

$$CD: \quad T_2 = \frac{\lambda_2 x}{l} \Rightarrow 2mg = \frac{\frac{\lambda_2 l}{2}}{l} \Rightarrow \lambda_2 = 4mg \qquad \dots ②$$

Figure 3.5

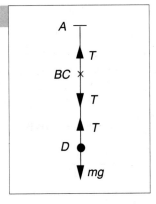

The point is that since the system is in equilibrium, the tension throughout the string is the same. Let this tension be T where $T = mg$.

To find the total extension, we'll find the extension in each part.

AB: $T = mg = \dfrac{\lambda_1 x_1}{l} = \dfrac{2mg\, x_1}{l}$ using ① $\Rightarrow x_1 = \dfrac{l}{2}$ ...③

CD: $T = mg = \dfrac{\lambda_2 x_2}{l} = \dfrac{4mg\, x_2}{l}$ using ② $\Rightarrow x_2 = \dfrac{l}{4}$ ...④

From ③ and ④ the total extension $x_1 + x_2 = \dfrac{l}{2} + \dfrac{l}{4} = \dfrac{3l}{4}$

Questions involving elastic strings usually combine this with some other topic such as circular motion or simple harmonic motion. Here is a final example of a static system and then we shall move on to systems involving a moving particle where we equate sums of three different kinds of energy.

Example

A thin uniform rod AB, of length 3 m and mass 5 kg, is freely pivoted to a fixed point A. A light elastic string BC, of modulus 30 N, has one end C fixed to a point at the same level as A, where $AC = 5$ m. When the system is in equilibrium, $\angle ABC = 90°$. Calculate:

(a)   the tension, in N, in the string

(b)   the natural length of the string.

Solution   Look at Figure 3.6

Figure 3.6

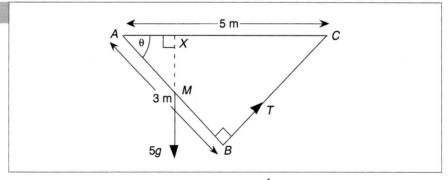

$\triangle\,ABC$ is $3 - 4 - 5$ and we can call the angle $B\hat{A}C\ \theta$.

Taking moments about the point A means that we don't have to worry about the reaction at the pivot. Since we are given that $A\hat{B}C = 90°$, the perpendicular distance of the line of action of the tension will be AB, i.e. 3 m. We now need the perpendicular distance of the line of action of the weight of the rod from A, which is marked AX in the diagram. Since AM will be $\dfrac{1}{2}AB$ for a uniform rod, $AM = \dfrac{3}{2}$ m and $AX = \dfrac{3}{2}\cos\theta$.

Since from the triangle, $\cos\theta = \dfrac{3}{5}$, $AX = \dfrac{3}{2}\times\dfrac{3}{5} = \dfrac{9}{10}$.

Now we can take moments about A:

$$T \times 3 - 5g \times \frac{9}{10} = 0$$

(a) $\quad 3T = 5g \times \frac{9}{10} \Rightarrow 3T = 45 \qquad$ (taking g to be 10 m s^{-2})

$$\Rightarrow T = 15 \text{ N}$$

(b) $\quad T = \frac{\lambda x}{l} \Rightarrow 15 = \frac{30x}{l} \Rightarrow x = \frac{l}{2}$

This is the extension, so the total stretched length, BC, will be $\frac{3l}{2}$.

Since $BC = 4$,

$$\frac{3l}{2} = 4 \Rightarrow l = \frac{8}{3} \text{ m}$$

You should now be able to answer Exercises 3–5 on pp. 42–43.

Energy stored in an elastic string

We have already seen how the **tension** in a stretched elastic string is given by the formula:

$$T = \frac{\lambda x}{l}$$

where λ is the modulus of elasticity of the string, x is the extension and l is the natural length.

A certain amount of **work** is necessary to produce this extension and so the **energy** that is stored in the stretched string must have the same magnitude as the work. To find the work done by a variable force, we integrate the force with respect to the distance,

i.e. work done = energy stored = $\int F \, ds$

Since the force is the tension and the distance expressed in x, the work done in extending from O to x is

$$\int_0^x T \, dx = \int_0^x \frac{\lambda x}{l} \, dx = \frac{\lambda x^2}{2l}$$

This is the result that we shall be using repeatedly in this section:

Energy stored in an elastic string is $\dfrac{\lambda x^2}{2l}$

If there are no external forces acting on a system and no friction or resistance to overcome, using energy to do so, no energy is lost, i.e. the total amount of energy remains the same. In the systems that we shall be looking at there are three types of energy making up the total energy:

- **kinetic energy**, from the movement of the mass(es)

- **potential energy**, from the position of the mass(es)

- **elastic energy**, stored in the stretched elastic string.

So by the principle of conservation of energy:

> The sum of the kinetic, potential and elastic energies
> at any position of the system is constant.

In practice, we make a table giving these energies at the positions we are interested in and use the principle above to set up our equation(s) in the unknown(s). Let's take a simple example and see how this works.

Example

A particle of mass 2 kg is attached to one end of an elastic string of natural length 2 m and modulus of elasticity 19.6 N. The other end of the elastic string is attached to the point A. If the particle is released from rest at the point A, find the greatest distance it will reach vertically below A. (Take g to be 9.8 m s^{-2}.)

Solution

When the particle is at A, it is stationary and so it has no kinetic energy. The string is not stretched and so there is no elastic energy stored in the string. Finally, if we take A to be the level from which to measure the potential energy, there will be no potential energy either.

Figure 3.7

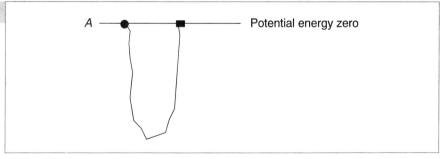

Our table for the energies is very simple!

	KE	PE	EE	Sum
At A	0	0	0	0

Now when the particle is released, it will increase in speed until it reaches the natural length of the string. From then on, there will be an increasing force from the tension in the stretched string which opposes the motion and eventually will bring the particle to a stop. This is the greatest distance it will fall below A – the tension then produces a movement upwards towards A again. To find this greatest distance we find what the energies will be at the instant when the particle comes temporarily to rest – we can call the point it reaches D and the distance AD we can call d.

Figure 3.8

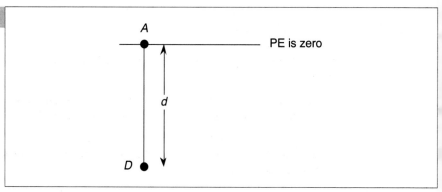

The particle is once again at rest, so there is no kinetic energy. It is **lower** than the zero level at A, so it has **lost** potential energy of magnitude $mgh = 2gd$ in this case. The string has a natural length of 2 m, so a distance of d between its ends represents an extension of $(d - 2)$, and so the elastic energy stored is:

$$\frac{\lambda x^2}{2l} = \frac{19.6 \times (d - 2)^2}{4}$$

Our table of energies would be

	KE	PE	EE
At D	0	$-2gd$	$\dfrac{19.6 \times (d - 2)^2}{4}$

and the sum of these must be the same as the sum at A, i.e. zero

$$-2gd + \frac{19.6 \times (d - 2)^2}{4} = 0$$

$$\frac{19.6(d - 2)^2}{4} = 2gd \quad \text{rearranging}$$

$$(d - 2)^2 = \frac{2 \times 9 \cdot 8 \times d \times 4}{19 \cdot 6}$$

i.e. $\quad d^2 - 4d + 4 = 4d$

$\quad\quad d^2 - 8d + 4 = 0$

$$d = \frac{8 \pm \sqrt{64 - 16}}{2} = 4 \pm \sqrt{12} = 4 \pm 2\sqrt{3}$$

If we take d to be $4 - 2\sqrt{3}$, it would mean that the distance fallen is less than the natural length of the string, which cannot be true. So the greatest distance below A is $(4 + 2\sqrt{3})$ m.

Here is another example with a particle being projected vertically upwards instead of dropping downwards.

Example

A light elastic string of natural length 5 m and modulus 4 N has one end fixed to a point O on level ground. To the other end of the string is attached a ball of mass 0.5 kg, which is projected vertically upwards from O with speed u m s^{-1}.

(a) Find u, given that the ball first comes to instantaneous rest when it reaches a height of 10 m above the ground.

(b) Given that the coefficient of restitution between the ball and the ground is 0.6, show that, after the first bounce at O, the string does not become taut.

Solution

We can fix the zero potential level at ground level, so that if the particle is above this level it has positive potential energy.

So initially, at ground level:

KE	PE	EE	Sum
$\frac{1}{2}mu^2$	0	0	$\frac{1}{2}mu^2$

When it has reached a height of 10 m above the ground,

Figure 3.9

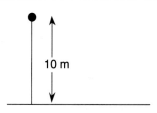

10 m

it comes to rest so its kinetic energy is zero. It has **gained** potential energy, $mgh = 0.5 \times g \times 10 = 5g$. It has also **gained** elastic energy. Since the string has a natural length of 5 m, a difference of 10 m between its ends means an extension of 5 m. Then the elastic energy, $\dfrac{1}{2}\dfrac{\lambda x^2}{l} = \dfrac{1}{2} \times \dfrac{4 \times 5^2}{5} = 10$ J

The sum of these energies is $5g + 10$ and since the initial sum of the energies was $\frac{1}{2}mu^2$,

$$\frac{1}{2}mu^2 = 5g + 10 = 59 \quad \text{(taking } g = 9.8 \text{ m s}^{-2}\text{)}$$

$$\Rightarrow u^2 = 4 \times 59 \Rightarrow u = 15.4 \text{ m s}^{-1} \text{ (1 d.p.)}$$

When it returns to ground level it will have this same velocity (only downwards) immediately **before** impact. Immediately **after** impact, its speed will be speed before $\times e = 15.4 \times 0.6 = 9.2$ m s^{-1} (1 d.p.) and so its kinetic energy will be $\frac{1}{2}mv^2 = 21.2$ J (1 d.p.).

In order to change all this kinetic energy to potential energy the particle would have to be at a height h given by

$$mgh = 21.2 \Rightarrow h = \frac{21.2}{mg} = 4.3 \text{ m}$$

At this height, all its kinetic energy would be exhausted, and since the natural length of the string 5 m, is more that this, it would not become taut.

You should now be able to answer Exercises 6–10 on pp. 43–44.

Particle on a plane

Exactly the same principle of conservation of energy applies if the particle, instead of falling vertically downwards, slides down an inclined plane. You have to be careful with the **potential** energy – the h in the formula mgh refers to the **vertical** height and not the distance down the face of the plane. Let's have a look at an example of this.

Example

One end of a light elastic string of modulus 20 mg and natural length a is attached to a point A on the surface of a smooth plane inclined at an angle of 30° to the horizontal. The other end is attached to a particle P of mass m. Initially P is held at rest at A and then released so that it slides down a line of greatest slope of the plane. By use of conservation of energy, or otherwise, show that the speed v of P when $AP = x$, ($x > a$), is given by

$$v^2 = \frac{g}{a}(41ax - 20a^2 - 20x^2).$$

(a) Find the maximum value of v in the subsequent motion.

(b) Find the maximum value of x in the subsequent motion.

Solution

Figure 3.10 illustrates this set-up.

Figure 3.10

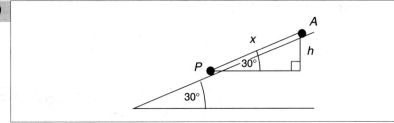

From the right-angled triangle we can find an expression for h, the vertical height fallen, in terms of x, the distance along the plane from A:

$$\sin 30° = \frac{h}{x} \Rightarrow h = x \sin 30° = \frac{x}{2}$$

If we call the potential energy at A zero, then each of the kinetic, potential and elastic energies are zero at A and so at any other point, the sum of these energies must also be zero.

If we call the speed of the particle at P, v, then its kinetic energy at this point will be $\frac{1}{2}mv^2$. There will have been a **loss** of potential energy of magnitude $mgh = mg\frac{x}{2}$ where x is the distance along the plane.

The extension in the string at this point will be $x - a$, where a is the natural length of the string, and so the elastic energy stored in the string will be:

$$\frac{1}{2}\lambda \frac{\text{Extension}^2}{l} \quad \text{i.e.} \quad \frac{1}{2} \times \frac{20mg\,(x-a)^2}{a}.$$

The sum of these three energies is zero, i.e.

$$\frac{1}{2}mv^2 - \frac{mg\,x}{2} + \frac{10mg\,(x-a)^2}{a} = 0$$

Rearranging, and dividing through by m,

$$\frac{1}{2}v^2 = \frac{gx}{2} - 10g\frac{(x-a)^2}{a}$$

$\times 2$ and collecting

$$v^2 = g\Big[x - 20\frac{(x-a)^2}{a}\Big] = \frac{g}{a}\Big[ax - 20(x-a)^2\Big]$$

$$= \frac{g}{a}\Big[ax - 20x^2 + 40ax - 20a^2\Big]$$

$$= \frac{g}{a}\Big[41ax - 20a^2 - 20x^2\Big] \qquad \text{...} \ ①$$

(a) We want to find the maximum value for v, so we want to find the value of x which makes $\frac{dv}{dx}$ zero. If we differentiate equation ① with respect to x, we get

$$2v\frac{dv}{dx} = \frac{g}{a}\Big[41a - 40x\Big] \quad (a \text{ is constant})$$

and if $\frac{dv}{dx}$ is zero, $41a - 40x = 0 \Rightarrow x = \frac{41a}{40}$

Putting this value of x into ①,

$$v^2 = \frac{g}{a}\Big[\frac{(41a)^2}{40} - 20a^2 - 20(\frac{41a}{40})^2\Big] = \frac{g}{a}\Big[\frac{(41a)^2}{40} - 20a^2 - \frac{(41a)^2}{80}\Big]$$

$$= \frac{g}{a}\left[\frac{(41a)^2}{80} - 20a^2\right] = \frac{g}{a}\left[\frac{(41a)^2 - 1600a^2}{80}\right]$$

$$= \frac{g \times 81a^2}{80a} = \frac{81ag}{80}$$

Then maximum value of v is $\sqrt{\frac{81ag}{80}} = \frac{9}{4}\sqrt{\frac{ag}{5}}$

(b)   The maximum value of x occurs when the **velocity** is zero, i.e. when

$$\frac{g}{a}(41ax - 20a^2 - 20x^2) = 0 \qquad \Rightarrow 20x^2 - 41ax + 20a^2 = 0$$

$$(5x - 4a)(4x - 5a) = 0 \qquad \Rightarrow x = \frac{4a}{5} \text{ or } x = \frac{5a}{4}$$

since we know that $x > a$, $\quad x = \frac{5a}{4}$

You should now be able to answer Exercises 11–13 on pp. 44–45.

Springs

The formulae for the tension and the stored energy in an elastic string are also true for springs except that the quantity x, which was just the extension in the elastic string, can now be either the **extension** or the **compression** in the spring. The working in the case of an extension of a spring is exactly the same as that of a string. Here's an example where the spring is compressed.

Example

A trolley of mass m runs down a smooth track of constant inclination $\frac{\pi}{6}$ to the horizontal, carrying at its front a light spring of natural length a and modulus $\frac{mga}{c}$, where c is constant. When the spring is fully compressed it is of length $\frac{a}{4}$, and it obeys Hooke's law up to this point. After the trolley has travelled a distance b from rest the spring meets a fixed stop. Show that, when the spring has been compressed a distance x, where $x < \frac{3a}{4}$, the speed v of the trolley is given by:

$$\frac{cv^2}{g} = c(b + x) - x^2.$$

Given that $c = \frac{a}{10}$ and $b = 2a$, find the total distance covered by the trolley before it momentarily comes to rest for the first time.

Solution	At the start of the motion, the kinetic and elastic energies are zero, and so if we take this to be the level from which we measure the potential energy, the total of the three energies will be zero.

Figure 3.11

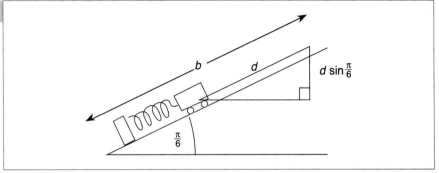

When it has travelled a distance d down the slope, the corresponding vertical distance is $d \sin \frac{\pi}{6} = \frac{d}{2}$ and so the loss in potential energy in this case will be $\frac{mgd}{2}$.

It meets the stop after it has travelled a distance of b down the slope and the spring is then compressed a further distance x, so the total distance travelled down the slope is $b + x$.

This means a loss in potential energy of $\frac{mg(b + x)}{2}$ from the result in the previous paragraph with $d = b + x$.

The gain in elastic potential energy is $\frac{1}{2} \times \frac{x^2}{l}$, i.e. $\frac{1}{2} \times \frac{mga}{c} \times \frac{x^2}{a} = \frac{mgx^2}{2c}$.

The gain in kinetic energy is $\frac{1}{2} mv^2$, and so, using the fact that the sum of the energies is zero,

$$-\frac{mg(b + x)}{2} + \frac{mgx^2}{2c} + \frac{mv^2}{2} = 0$$

Rearranging, $\dfrac{v^2}{2} = \dfrac{g(b + x)}{2} - \dfrac{gx^2}{2c}$ multiplying by $\dfrac{2c}{g}$

$$\frac{cv^2}{g} = c(b + x) - x^2$$

When it comes to rest, $v = 0 \Rightarrow c(b + x) - x^2 = 0$.

$c = \dfrac{a}{10}$ and $b = 2a \Rightarrow \dfrac{a}{10}(2a + x) - x^2 = 0$

$2a^2 + ax - 10x^2 = 0$

$10x^2 - ax - 2a^2 = 0$

$$(5x + 2a)(2x - a) = 0 \implies x = \frac{a}{2}, \text{ taking the positive solution,}$$

and total distance, $b + x$ is $\dfrac{5a}{2}$

You should now be able to answer Exercise 14 on p. 45.

EXERCISES

1 Find the extension when a particle of mass 2 kg is suspended on one end of an elastic string of natural length 3 m and modulus of elasticity $12g$ N.

2 Find the modulus of elasticity of an elastic string of natural length 0.5 m if a mass of 500 g suspended on one end produces an extension of 0.05 m.

3 The figure shows an elastic string AB, of natural length $4l$. The end A is fixed and the other end B carries a particle of mass m. The particle is held at a horizontal distance $4l$ from the vertical through A by a horizontal force kmg, which acts in the vertical plane through the stretched string.

When the particle rests in this position, the length of the string is $5l$. Show that the modulus of elasticity of the string is $\dfrac{20mg}{3}$ and calculate the tension in the string and the numerical value of k.

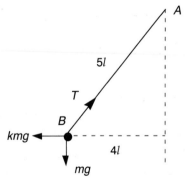

4 Two light elastic strings AB and CD, each with the same natural length c, have moduli of elasticity $9mg$ and $12mg$ respectively. The ends B and C are joined together, the end A is tied at a fixed point and a particle of mass M is attached to D. The particle hangs in equilibrium with the strings vertical. Find, in terms of c the length of AD.

5 A uniform rod AB, of length $4l$ and weight W, is smoothly hinged at its end A to a vertical wall. A light string attaches the other end B to a fixed point C on the wall vertically above A, where $AC = 3l$. Given that the rod rests in equilibrium with $AB = BC$, show by taking moments about A, or otherwise, that the tension in the string is $\frac{2W}{3}$.

Given that the string is elastic and of natural length $3l$, state its modulus of elasticity.

A particle of weight k is now suspended from the rod at B. Given that the rod rests in equilibrium with AB horizontal, find k.

6 A light elastic string AB has natural length l m and modulus of elasticity λ N. The end A is attached to a fixed point. When B is held at rest at a distance 0.6 m from A, the tension in the string is 3 N.

(a) Find an equation relating λ and l.

When B is held at rest at a distance 0.7 m from A, the elastic energy in the string is 0.6 J.

(b) Show that $l = 0.5$ and find the value of λ.

7 A light elastic string, of natural length c and modulus of elasticity $4\,mg$, is attached at one end to a fixed point A. A particle of mass m is tied to the other end B of the string.

(a) If the particle hangs in equilibrium, calculate the length AB of the extended string.

(b) If the particle is held at A and allowed to fall vertically, use the principle of conservation of energy to find the greatest distance between A and B in the ensuing motion.

8 A particle of mass m is suspended from a fixed point O by a light elastic string of natural length l. When the mass is hanging freely at rest the length of the string is $\frac{13l}{12}$. The particle is allowed to fall from rest at O. Find the greatest extension of the string in the subsequent motion. Show that the maximum kinetic energy of the particle during this fall occurs when it passes through the equilibrium position.

9 One end of a light elastic string, of natural length a and modulus of elasticity $3mg$, is fixed at a point A and the other end carries a particle P of mass m. The particle is held at A and then projected vertically down with speed $\sqrt{3ga}$. Find the distance AP when the acceleration of the particle is instantaneously zero.

Find also the maximum speed attained by the particle during its motion.

10 Show that the work done in stretching a light elastic string by a length x from its natural length a is $\frac{1}{2}Tx$, where T is the final tension in the string.

One end A of a light elastic string AB of natural length a is attached to a fixed point at a height $a + b$ above a horizontal floor, where $b > 0$. To the other end B is attached a small spherical ball of mass m.

The modulus of elasticity of the string is $\frac{mga}{b}$.

(a) Show that in equilibrium under gravity the ball is just in contact with the floor.

The ball is released from rest at A.

(b) Show that it strikes the floor with speed v, given by
$$v^2 = (2a + b)g.$$

When the ball strikes the floor the elastic string breaks and the ball rebounds to a height a.

(c) Find, in terms of a and b, the coefficient of restitution between the ball and the floor.

11 (In Exercises 11 and 12, take acceleration due to gravity to be 10 m s^{-2}.)

One end of a light elastic string of natural length 0.5 m and modulus of elasticity 40 N is attached to a fixed point A. The other end of the string is attached to a particle P of mass 1 kg. The particle is held at A and is released from rest. The speed of P when at a distance s metres below A is $v \text{ m s}^{-1}$.

(a) Write down an expression for v^2 in terms of s when $s \le 0.5$.

(b) When $s > 0.5$ show that $v^2 = 100s - 80s^2 - 20$.

Find the value of s for which the speed is greatest, and find also the greatest value of s attained during the motion.

Calculate the two values of s for which $v = 2.5$.

12 An elastic string has unstretched length a and modulus of elasticity λ. Show that, when the extension of the string is x, the elastic potential energy stored in the string is $\frac{\lambda x^2}{2a}$.

Fixed points A and B are at the same horizontal level and are 1.5 m apart. A particle P of mass 2 kg is attached to A and B by means of two light elastic strings AP and BP, each of which has unstretched length 0.75 m and modulus of elasticity 48 N. The particle is held at the mid-point of AB and is released from rest. Calculate the speed of P when it has fallen 1 m.

The equilibrium position of P vertically below the mid-point of AB is such that $A\hat{P}B = 2\theta$. Prove that: $\cot\theta - \cos\theta = \frac{5}{24}$.

13 A small bead *B* of mass 0.1 kg is free to slide on a smooth fixed vertical rod *AV*. One end of a light elastic string of modulus 12 N and natural length 1 m is attached to *B* and the other end is attached to a fixed point *O* which is at a perpendicular distance of 1.2 m from *AV*.

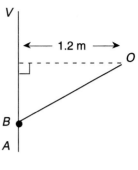

The bead is released from rest from the position where *OB* is horizontal. Show that when *B* has dropped a distance of 0.5 m the energy stored in the string has increased by 0.3 J and find the speed of *B* at this time.

(Take *g* to be 10 m s^{-2}.)

14 A small cubical block of mass 8*m* is attached to one end *A* of a light elastic spring *AB* of natural length 3*a* and modulus of elasticity 6*mg*. The spring and block are at rest on a smooth horizontal table with *AB* equal to 3*a* and lying perpendicularly to the face to which *A* is attached. A second block of equal physical dimensions, but of mass *m*, moving with a speed $(2ga)^{\frac{1}{2}}$ in the direction parallel to *BA* impinges on the free end *B* of the spring.

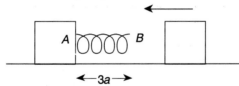

Assuming that the heavier block is held fixed and that *AB* remains straight and horizontal in the subsequent motion, determine the maximum compression of the spring.

SUMMARY

This section has covered the mathematics behind systems involving elastic strings, both in equilibrium and in motion. You should now :

● know the formula for the tension in an extended elastic string and be able to apply it to static situations

● know the formula for the elastic potential energy in an extended elastic string and use this, together with the principle of conservation of mechanical energy, to find unknowns in dynamic situations.

● know that the greatest speed of a particle falling on the end of an elastic string occurs when it passes through the equilibrium position

● know that at the greatest depth, the velocity of the particle is instantaneously zero.

4

Uniform circular motion

In this section we are going to look at the motion of a particle that describes a horizontal circle and the force that is necessary to keep it in this path. This is quite a large topic because there are so many variations on a basic theme. The examples and exercises have been chosen so that when you have completed the section you will have met the more common types and should have picked up enough of the general principles to be able to tackle successfully other questions.

In order to work through this section you should be familiar with:

- radian measure
- resolving forces.

Linear and angular velocity

The speed of the particle travelling round the circle can be measured in two ways – either the familiar **linear** measure, i.e. so many centimetres or metres in a second, or **angular** measure, i.e. so many **revolutions** per second (rev s^{-1}) or so many **radians** per second (rad s^{-1}).

The conversion from revolutions to radians per second and vice versa is quite straightforward – since there are 2π radians in one revolution, we divide or multiply by the factor 2π as appropriate. For example:

$$4 \text{ rev s}^{-1} \equiv 8\pi \text{ rad s}^{-1}$$

$$\frac{3}{\pi} \text{ rev s}^{-1} \equiv \frac{3}{\pi} \times 2\pi = 6 \text{ rad s}^{-1}$$

and conversely

$$2 \text{ rad s}^{-1} \equiv \frac{2}{2\pi} = \frac{1}{\pi} \text{ rev s}^{-1}$$

$$10\pi \text{ rad s}^{-1} \equiv 5 \text{ rev s}^{-1}$$

To convert between linear, e.g. m s^{-1}, and angular, rad s^{-1}, we have to remember the formula for arc length, i.e. arc length = $r\theta$ where r is the radius in metres and θ the angle in radians. This is illustrated in Figure 4.1.

Figure 4.1

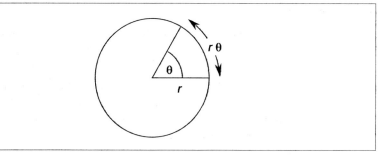

This means that when the particle has turned through an angle of θ radians, it has travelled a distance around the circle of rθ, i.e.

Angular θ rad s⁻¹ ≡ linear r θ m s⁻¹

Conventionally we use the greek letter ω for angular velocity just as we usually use *v* for linear velocity, and then in appropriate units

v = rω

This means that the linear velocity increases as the radius of the circle increases – so that, for example, you have to run faster on the outside of a running track to keep up with someone on the inside lane.

The period of revolution

The period of revolution is the term that describes how long it takes to go once round the circle.

1   If the speed is given as R rev s⁻¹, then the time for 1 revolution is simply $\frac{1}{R}$ seconds.

2   If the speed is given as ω rad s⁻¹, we want the time for 1 revolution, i.e. 2π radians, which will be:

$$\frac{2\pi}{\omega} \text{ seconds} \left(\text{as in Time} = \frac{\text{Distance}}{\text{Speed}} \right)$$

3   If the speed is given as v m s⁻¹, we want the time for one **circumference** of the circle, i.e. $2\pi r$, where r is the radius, which will be:

$$\frac{2\pi r}{v} \text{ seconds}$$

You should now be able to answer Exercises 1–3 on p. 68.

Central force

Unless a force of some kind is acting, a particle in motion will continue at the same velocity along a straight line. When a particle is moving in a circle it's being forced all the time inwards, away from a straight path.

In Figure 4.2, the particle at P_1 would keep going in a straight line if there were no force acting, but it continues along the circle to P_2 under the action of the central force, F. This force has to continue to act for the particle to pass around the circle to P_3 and so on.

Figure 4.2

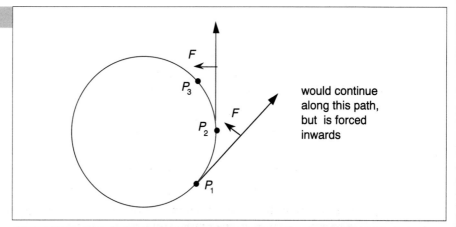

The **magnitude** of this force has to be

$$mr\omega^2 \text{ or } \frac{mv^2}{r}$$

and it is always directed towards the **centre** of the circle.

This means that if we know two of (a) the force, (b) the radius and (c) the speed, we can calculate the value of the remaining unknown quantity.

Example A particle of mass m kg is moving in a horizontal circle under the action of a force of magnitude $45m$ N directed towards the centre of the circle. If the radius of the circle is 5 m, find the angular velocity.

Solution We have to examine the question first of all to find out which of the forms for the force is applicable. Here we want **angular** velocity, so we use the formula $F = mr\omega^2$.

Then $mr\omega^2 = 45m$ and $r = 5$

$5\omega^2 = 45$

$\omega^2 = 9$ $\Rightarrow$ $\omega = 3$ rad s^{-1}

| **Example** | A force of 12.5 N acts on a particle of mass 2 kg in such a way that the particle describes a horizontal circle of radius 4 m with constant speed. Find the time for 1 revolution correct to 1 decimal place. |

| **Solution** | We can use either of the forms in this case. Taking the one for linear speed, |

$$F = \frac{mv^2}{r} = 12.5$$

Putting $m = 2$ and $r = 4$,

$$\frac{2v^2}{4} = 12.5$$

$$\Rightarrow v^2 = 25 \text{ and } v = 5 \text{ m s}^{-1}$$

Since the circumference is $2\pi r = 8\pi$, it will take

$$\frac{8\pi}{5} = 5.0 \text{ seconds (1 d.p.)}$$

You should now be able to answer Exercises 4–5 on p. 69.

Now let's have a look at different systems where the force inwards can be provided by the tension in a string or the reaction between the particle and the surface on which it is rotating.

Conical pendulum

When a particle is attached to one end of a string, the other end of which is fixed, and the particle describes a horizontal circle, the string traces out the shape of a cone and the system is called a **conical pendulum**.

| **Figure 4.3** | 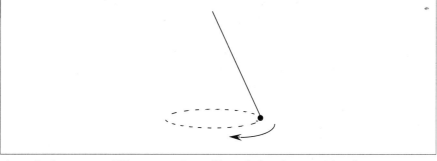 |

A typical system will have a string of length l and a particle of mass m at one end. To simplify matters, we can draw it in two dimensions, and then mark in the forces that are acting on the particle. To complete the diagram we can draw in the vertical from the fixed end and call the angle the string makes with this vertical θ.

Figure 4.4

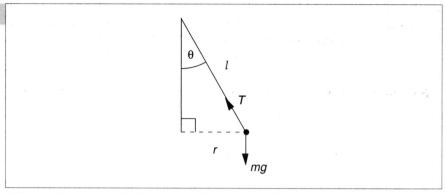

We can then generally find any unknowns in the system from **three** equations:

①   vertical

②   horizontal

③   triangle

and we'll look at each of these in turn.

Since the particle is moving in a **horizontal** circle there is no movement vertically, and so the vertical forces are in equilibrium, i.e.

$$T \cos \theta - mg = 0 \hspace{4cm} \text{... } ①$$

Also, since the motion is in a circle, there must be a force towards the centre of this circle of $\dfrac{mv^2}{r}$ (or $mr\omega^2$) and since the only force acting towards the centre is $T \sin \theta$,

$$T \sin \theta = \frac{mv^2}{r} \hspace{4cm} \text{... } ②$$

Finally, from the triangle,

$$\sin \theta = \frac{r}{l} \hspace{4cm} \text{... } ③$$

In fact, until we come to circular motion with **elastic** strings, these three basic equations, i.e. vertical, horizontal and triangle, will still be sufficient even when the system becomes more complicated. For the moment though, let's have a look at an example.

Example

A conical pendulum consists of a light inextensible string of length l with a particle of mass m attached to its free end. The particle describes a horizontal circle with angular speed ω and the string makes an angle of 60° with the vertical. Express l in terms of g and ω.

| Solution | Drawing a diagram and marking in the information given, the tension T and the radius r of the horizontal circle, we get Figure 4.5. |

Figure 4.5

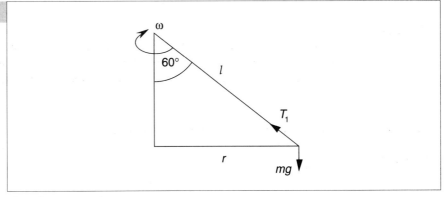

Our three equations are:

Vertical: $\quad T_1 \cos 60° = mg$ ... ①

Horizontal: $\quad T_1 \sin 60° = mr\omega^2$ ... ②

Δ: $\qquad\quad \sin 60° \;= \dfrac{r}{l}$ ... ③

From ①, since $\cos 60° = \dfrac{1}{2}$, $\dfrac{T_1}{2} = mg \;\Rightarrow\; T_1 = 2mg$ and substituting this into ② gives:

$$2mg \sin 60° = mr\omega^2 \quad \text{and since } \sin 60° = \frac{\sqrt{3}}{2}$$

$$mg\sqrt{3} = mr\omega^2 \quad \Rightarrow \quad r = \frac{g\sqrt{3}}{\omega^2} \qquad \text{... ④}$$

Using $\sin 60° = \dfrac{\sqrt{3}}{2}$ and putting ④ into ③:

$$\frac{\sqrt{3}}{2} = \frac{\dfrac{g\sqrt{3}}{\omega^2}}{l} \quad \Rightarrow \quad \frac{l}{2} = \frac{g}{\omega^2} \quad \Rightarrow \quad l = \frac{2g}{\omega^2} \qquad \text{... ⑤}$$

Motion on a horizontal surface

A possible question here is that of a particle on a rough horizontal turn-table, with the friction being the central force. Here is an example of this.

Example A coin is placed on the edge of a horizontal turntable with the centre of the coin 20 cm from the axis of rotation. The turntable is rotating at the rate of 45 revs per minute. By modelling the coin as a particle, calculate the least possible value for the coefficient of friction between the coin and the turntable.

Solution A suitable diagram is shown in Figure 4.6.

Figure 4.6

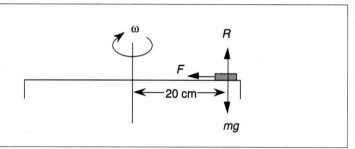

We first of all convert the rate of rotation into rads per second.

$$\omega = 45 \text{ revs min}^{-1} \equiv \frac{45}{60} \times 2\pi \text{ rads sec}^{-1}$$

i.e. $\omega = \dfrac{3\pi}{2} \text{ rads sec}^{-1}$ ... ①

Resolving vertically, $R = mg$ ... ②

Resolving horizontally, $F = mr\omega^2$ ... ③

Since $F \le \mu R$, $mr\omega^2 \le \mu mg$

$\Rightarrow r\omega^2 \le \mu g$

$$\Rightarrow \mu \ge \frac{r\omega^2}{g} = \frac{0.2 \times \left(\frac{3\pi}{2}\right)^2}{9.8} = 0.45$$

Apart from examples like this, the surface will be **smooth** in the questions you are likely to encounter for this module and so the only addition is a normal reaction from the surface which changes the equation for the vertical forces. A possible question in connection with this is to find the maximum speed for which the particle remains in contact with the table, i.e. find the condition that the normal reaction is greater than zero. Let's have a look at an example of this.

Example

As shown in Figure 4.7, a particle A of mass m is in contact with a smooth horizontal plane, and is attached by means of a light inextensible string to the fixed point O, which is at a height h above the plane. A moves in uniform circular motion in contact with the plane, and with the string taut.

Prove that the angular speed, ω, of the motion satisfies $\omega^2 < \dfrac{g}{h}$.

Figure 4.7

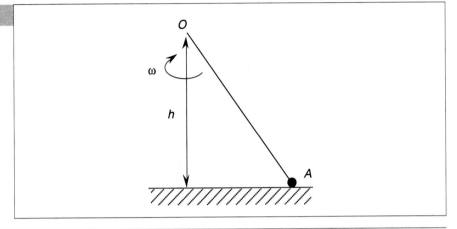

Solution

Redrawing the diagram with the forces acting on the particle A, marking the radius r of the circle and putting in θ, the angle the string makes with the downward vertical, we get Figure 4.8.

Figure 4.8

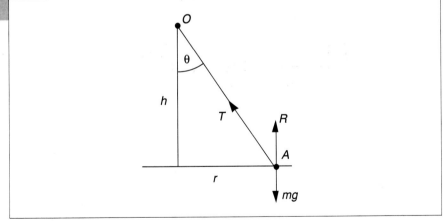

The three equations are:

$$\text{Vertical:} \qquad R + T \cos \theta = mg \qquad \qquad \dots \text{①}$$

$$\text{Horizontal:} \qquad T \sin \theta = mr\omega^2 \qquad \qquad \dots \text{②}$$

$$\Delta : \qquad \tan \theta = \frac{r}{h} \qquad \qquad \dots \text{③}$$

Note the addition of the normal reaction R in equation ①.

Rearranging ① to give $T \cos \theta = mg - R$ and dividing this into ② gives:

$$\frac{T \sin \theta}{T \cos \theta} = \frac{mr\omega^2}{mg - R}$$

i.e. $\tan \theta = \dfrac{mr\omega^2}{mg - R}$ ... ④

With ③, this becomes $\dfrac{r}{h} = \dfrac{mr\omega^2}{mg - R}$

which becomes $mg - R = mh\omega^2 \quad \Rightarrow \quad R = mg - mh\omega^2$ ... ⑤

Now we apply the condition that the particle should remain on the table, i.e. $R > 0$ and then

$$mg - mh\omega^2 > 0$$
$$\Rightarrow mh\omega^2 < mg$$

i.e. $\omega^2 < \dfrac{g}{h}$ since $h > 0$ and $m > 0$

You should now be able to answer Exercises 6–8 on p. 69.

Smooth beads

We are now going to look at slightly more involved systems where the particle, a bead or ring for example, is free to slide along a single string. We'll look at the former case first.

When the bead is **smooth** and can take any position on the string, the tension throughout the string is the same. The three equations that we used for the previous examples are still usually sufficient to solve the new system – there will be slight changes to the vertical and horizontal equations since there may be a component from *each* of the strings in these directions. There can be a little extra geometry involved sometimes to find the fraction of the string on either side of the bead. Let's have a look at a typical problem of this sort.

Example   One end of a light inextensible string of length $2c$ is attached at a fixed point A and the other end is attached at a fixed point B, where B is at a distance c vertically above A. A smooth ring of mass m is threaded on the string and made to rotate in a horizontal circle, centre A, with constant speed. Show that the tension in the string is $\dfrac{5mg}{4}$ and calculate the speed of the ring.

Solution

Be careful to read the question carefully with examples of this kind – it's very easy to misinterpret the information given and start off with the wrong diagram.

Figure 4.9

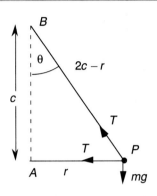

Since the length of the string is $2c$, if we call AP r then BP will be $2c - r$.

Vertically: $T \cos \theta - mg = 0$ ... ①

Horizontally: $T + T \sin \theta = \dfrac{mv^2}{r}$ ... ②

Δ: $\cos \theta = \dfrac{c}{2c - r}$ ... ③

There is actually an additional equation from the triangle in this case. Using Pythagoras,

$$(2c - r)^2 = c^2 + r^2$$
$$4c^2 - 4cr + r^2 = c^2 + r^2$$
$$3c^2 - 4cr = 0$$
$$\Rightarrow r = \dfrac{3c}{4}$$ ... ④

Putting this back into ③, $\cos \theta = \dfrac{c}{2c - \dfrac{3c}{4}} = \dfrac{c}{\dfrac{5c}{4}} = \dfrac{4}{5}$ ... ⑤

and this into ① gives $T \times \dfrac{4}{5} - mg = 0$

$$\Rightarrow T = \dfrac{5mg}{4}$$ ... ⑥

If $\cos \theta = \dfrac{4}{5}$ $\sin \theta = \dfrac{3}{5}$

55

and ② becomes $T + T \times \dfrac{3}{5} = \dfrac{mv^2}{r}$

Putting in the values of T and r from ④ and ⑥,

$$\frac{5mg}{4}\left(1 + \frac{3}{5}\right) = \frac{mv^2}{\dfrac{3c}{4}}$$

$$v^2 = \frac{3c}{4} \times \frac{5g}{4}\left(\frac{8}{5}\right) = \frac{3cg}{2}$$

i.e. $v = \sqrt{\dfrac{3gc}{2}}$

Two strings

There is little difference if the particle is supported by two strings – the same three basic equations are enough to solve the system. Remember that the tensions in the two strings are *different*, so they should be labelled T_1 and T_2, for example (as opposed to the previous section where the tensions either side of a smooth bead were the same).

Example   Figure 4.10 shows a particle of mass m which is attached to fixed points A and B by means of two light inextensible strings of lengths l and $l\sqrt{3}$ respectively. B is a distance l vertically above A. The system rotates with constant angular speed ω about AB, and both strings are taut.

Figure 4.10

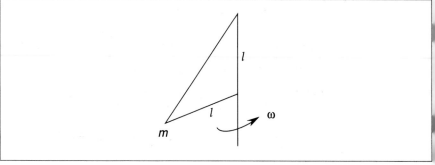

(a)   Show that the strings make angles of 60° and 30° with the vertical.

(b)   Find expressions in terms of m, g, ω and l for the tensions in the strings.

(c)   Show that $\dfrac{2g}{3l} < \omega^2 < \dfrac{2g}{l}$.

| **Solution** | Putting in all the information, we get Figure 4.11: |

Figure 4.11

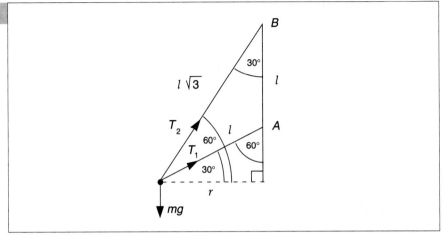

(a) By the cos rule, $\cos \hat{B} = \dfrac{l^2 + 3l^2 - l^2}{2 \times l \times l\sqrt{3}} = \dfrac{3}{2\sqrt{3}} = \dfrac{\sqrt{3}}{2} \Rightarrow \hat{B} = 30°$

Since the upper triangle is isosceles, the obtuse angle at A will be $120°$ and so the angle that the lower string makes will be $180° - 120°$, i.e. $60°$.

(b) Forces on the particle,

vertical : $\qquad T_2 \cos 30° + T_1 \cos 60° - mg = 0 \qquad \qquad \ldots ①$

horizontal : $\qquad T_2 \sin 30° + T_1 \sin 60° = mr\omega^2 \qquad \qquad \ldots ②$

lower Δ : $\qquad \cos 30° = \dfrac{r}{l} \qquad \qquad \ldots ③$

Using $\cos 30° = \dfrac{\sqrt{3}}{2}$, ③ becomes $r = \dfrac{l\sqrt{3}}{2}$ and putting this into ② together with the values for the trig. ratios

$$T_2 \times \frac{1}{2} + T_1 \times \frac{\sqrt{3}}{2} = m \times \frac{l\sqrt{3}}{2} \times \omega^2$$

i.e. $\qquad \qquad T_2 + T_1 \sqrt{3} = ml\omega^2\sqrt{3} \qquad \qquad \ldots ④$

and similarly ① becomes $\qquad T_2 \times \dfrac{\sqrt{3}}{2} + T_1 \times \dfrac{1}{2} - mg = 0$

i.e. $\quad T_2 \sqrt{3} + T_1 = 2mg \qquad \qquad \ldots ⑤$

$\qquad T_2 \sqrt{3} + 3T_1 = 3ml\omega^2$

$\qquad 2T_1 = 3ml\omega^2 - 2mg \qquad ④ \times \sqrt{3} - ⑤$

i.e $\quad T_1 = \dfrac{m}{2}\left[3l\omega^2 - 2g\right]$ and this into ⑤ gives

$$T_2 \sqrt{3} = 2mg - \frac{3ml\omega^2}{2} + mg = \frac{3m}{2}\left[2g - l\omega^2\right]$$

i.e. $\quad T_2 = \frac{m\sqrt{3}}{2}\left[2g - l\omega^2\right]$

(c) Since both strings are taut, T_1 and T_2 are greater than zero

$$T_1 > 0 \implies \frac{m}{2}\left[3l\omega^2 - 2g\right] > 0$$

$$\implies 3l\omega^2 - 2g > 0 \implies \omega^2 > \frac{2g}{3l}$$

$$T_2 > 0 \implies \frac{m\sqrt{3}}{2}\left[2g - l\omega^2\right] > 0$$

$$\implies 2g - l\omega^2 > 0 \implies \omega^2 < \frac{2g}{l}$$

Combining these two, $\quad \dfrac{2g}{3l} < \omega^2 < \dfrac{2g}{l}$

You should now be able to answer Exercises 9–10 on pp. 69–70.

Two particles

The final variation on this type of system where the string is **inelastic** is the addition of an extra particle fastened on to the other end of the string.

Questions can be set where the string has a particle at each end, one of which is stationary and the other of which is describing a horizontal circle. The force on the stationary particle which opposes the tension and maintains equilibrium comes either from its weight if hanging or from friction if supported by a rough horizontal plane.

Figure 4.12

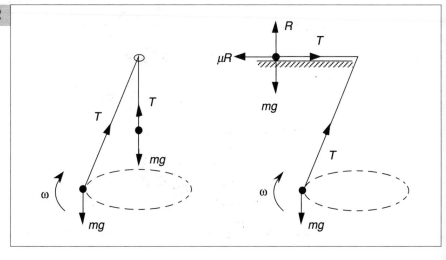

We will need at least one, and possibly two, additional equation(s) which come from looking at the equilibrium of the stationary particle. Here's an example of the first type, where the stationary particle is hanging.

Example

A light inextensible string, of length 2 m, passes through a small fixed smooth ring R and carries particle A, of mass $2M$, at one end and particle B, of mass M, at the other end. The particle A is at rest vertically below R. The particle B moves in a horizontal circle, the centre of which is vertically below R, with constant angular speed 4 rad s^{-1}. Given that the string remains taut, calculate the distance AR. (Take g as 10 m s^{-2}.)

Solution

It's quite easy to make mistakes in questions of this kind, so once you've drawn your diagram, check back that the information in the question fits. We'll mark in θ, the angle that the string makes with the downward vertical, as in Figure 4.13.

Figure 4.13

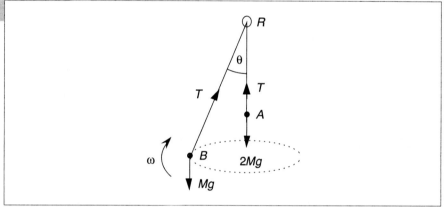

Since A is stationary, the forces in A are in equilibrium, i.e.

$$T - 2Mg = 0 \qquad \qquad \dots \text{①}$$

For the particle B,

Vertically: $T \cos \theta - Mg = 0$ $\qquad \dots \text{②}$

Horizontally: $T \sin \theta = Mr\omega^2$ $\qquad \dots \text{③}$

From the triangle shown in Figure 4.14, $\sin \theta = \dfrac{r}{l}$. $\qquad \dots \text{④}$

Figure 4.14

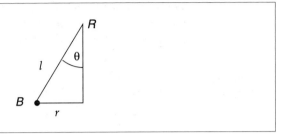

In fact, in this example we don't need all these equations.

Combining ③ and ④,

$$\frac{Tr}{l} = Mr\omega^2 \qquad \Rightarrow l = \frac{T}{M\omega^2} \qquad \qquad \dots ⑤$$

But from ①, $T = 2Mg$ and so

$$l = \frac{2Mg}{M\omega^2} \quad \text{and since } \omega = 4 \text{ (given)}$$

$$l = \frac{2g}{16} = \frac{5}{4}\, \text{m}$$

This is the distance BR, so $AR = 2 - \dfrac{5}{4} = \dfrac{3}{4}\, \text{m}$

Other systems involving circular motion

That concludes the subsection dealing with circular motion involving an inelastic string. We are now going to look at three other types of system which appear very different but where, in fact, the same general principles can be carried over with little change necessary in the basic equations.

Bead in a bowl

The first of these is where the particle is moving in a horizontal circle around the inside of a hemispherical shape, a bowl for instance, and the force towards the centre of the circle is provided by the component of the normal reaction in this direction.

Figure 4.15

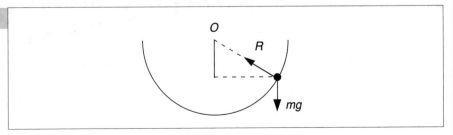

There is in fact very little difference between this and a conical pendulum – the same three equations apply, with the normal reaction (which passes through the centre of the circle) appearing instead of a tension. Here's an example.

Example

A particle P, moving on the smooth inside surface of a fixed hemispherical bowl, of radius r, describes a horizontal circle at depth $\dfrac{r}{2}$ below the centre of the bowl. Show that P takes time $\pi\sqrt{\dfrac{2r}{g}}$ to complete one revolution of its circular path.

Solution

If we call the mass of the particle m and the normal reaction of the particle on the smooth surface R, we have the following system:

Figure 4.16

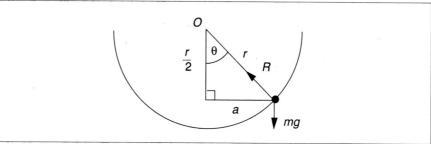

Vertically: $R \cos \theta = mg$ ... ①

Horizontally: $R \sin \theta = ma\omega^2$ ... ②

Δ: $\cos \theta = \dfrac{\frac{r}{2}}{r} = \dfrac{1}{2}$

i.e. $\theta = 60°$ ... ③

Putting this into ①, $R \cos 60° = mg$

$\Rightarrow R = 2mg$ ... ④

Also from the triangle, $\sin \theta = \dfrac{a}{r}$, and putting this together with ④ into ②,

$$2mg \times \dfrac{a}{r} = ma\omega^2 \quad \Rightarrow \omega^2 = \dfrac{2g}{r}$$

$\therefore \qquad \omega = \sqrt{\dfrac{2g}{r}}$ rad s^{-1}

The time for 1 revolution, i.e. 2π radians, will be:

$$\dfrac{2\pi}{\sqrt{\dfrac{2g}{r}}} = \pi\sqrt{\dfrac{2r}{g}}$$

Here's another example of circular motion, this time on a slightly larger scale.

Satellites in orbit

When an object like a satellite is orbiting the earth, the force that stops it flying out into space is the gravitational 'pull' of the earth. If we know an expression for this, we can connect the height and speed of the object and find the time for one revolution.

Example

The motion of an artificial satellite may be assumed to be uniform motion in a circle whose centre is at the centre of the earth, and the centre of the earth may be regarded as a fixed point. The gravitational force exerted by the earth on any object of mass m is inversely proportional to the square of the distance of the object from the centre of the earth, and at the earth's surface this force is mg.

Prove that a satellite orbiting at a height h above the earth's surface completes one revolution in time T, where

$$T^2 = \frac{4\pi^2(R + h)^3}{gR^2}$$

and where R is the radius of the earth.

Solution

The distance of the centre of the earth from the satellite is $R + h$ (see Figure 4.17) and so the gravitational force of the earth on the satellite will be:

$$F = \frac{k}{(R + h)^2} \qquad \dots \text{①}$$

Figure 4.17

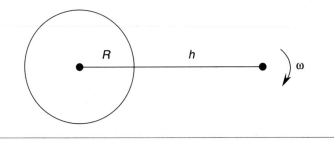

But we're told that on the surface of the earth, i.e. $h = 0$, this force is mg, i.e.

$$mg = \frac{k}{(R + 0)^2} = \frac{k}{R^2} \Rightarrow k = mgR^2 \qquad \dots \text{②}$$

Putting this back into ①

$$F = \frac{mg\,R^2}{(R + h)^2} \qquad \dots \text{③}$$

But this force is responsible for the circular motion, i.e. $F = mr\omega^2$, where r is the radius of the circle. But this is $R + h$ and so

$$F = m(R + h)\omega^2 \qquad \qquad \dots ④$$

Equating ③ and ④,

$$\frac{mgR^2}{(R + h)^2} = m(R + h)\omega^2$$

i.e. $\qquad \omega^2 = \frac{gR^2}{(R + h)^3} \qquad \qquad \dots ⑤$

But the time T for one revolution is $\dfrac{2\pi}{\omega}$,

$$T = \frac{2\pi}{\omega} \Rightarrow T^2 = \frac{4\pi^2}{\omega^2} \qquad \qquad \dots ⑥$$

Inserting ⑤ into ⑥,

$$T^2 = \frac{4\pi^2(R + h)^3}{gR^2}$$

For the final of these three variants of circular motion, we move back down to a smaller scale.

Bead on a rotating wire

If a bead is threaded on a circular wire and the wire rotates around a vertical diameter, the bead will describe a circle provided that it stays in the same place relative to the wire.

Figure 4.18

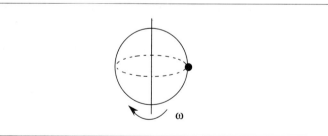

If the wire is smooth the force towards the centre will be provided by the normal reaction between the bead and the wire, which passes through the centre of the wire circle. For the bead to remain stationary relative to the wire, the vertical component of the reaction and the weight have to balance.

Figure 4.19

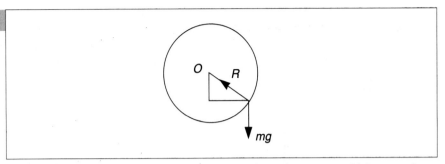

With a **rough** wire, the friction can act in either of two ways. If the angular velocity is not very large, the bead will tend to drop towards the bottom of the wire and the friction, opposing this tendency, will act **upwards**. As the angular velocity increases there will be a speed at which the bead remains in equilibrium relative to the wire.

A further increase in angular velocity means that the bead will tend to slip upwards and the friction will then act **downwards**.

You should now be able to answer Exercises 11–12 on pp. 70–71.

Elastic strings

The next part of this section deals with particles on an *elastic* string. This topic is frequently found in exam questions, together with parts dealing simply with extension in static situations or elastic stored energy in dynamic situations.

When the string supporting the particle describing the horizontal circle is **elastic**, we can find an expression for the tension from the formula for an elastic string, $T = \dfrac{\lambda x}{l}$ and this, together with the usual equations for circular motion, should mean that we can solve the system.

Let's have a look at a couple of examples of this, the first of which is quite straightforward.

Example   A particle is suspended from a fixed point by a light elastic string of natural length a. In equilibrium the length of the string is $\dfrac{3a}{2}$. The particle is set rotating in a horizontal circle with uniform speed, the string being at a constant angle to the vertical and extended to a length $2a$. Find the speed of the particle.

Solution We're not told the mass of the particle nor the modulus of elasticity of the string, so we'll call them m and λ as usual. Our first equation comes from looking at the particle in equilibrium, as shown in Figure 4.20.

Figure 4.20

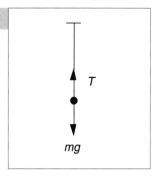

i.e. $T - mg = 0$ ... ①

Also, since the string is elastic,

$$T = \frac{\lambda x}{l}$$ ... ②

and we're told that the length is now $\frac{3a}{2}$, i.e. $x = \frac{a}{2}$ and $l = a$

so that ② becomes:

$$T = \frac{\lambda}{a} \times \frac{a}{2} = \frac{\lambda}{2}$$ ... ③

Since from ①, $T = mg$, we have:

$$mg = \frac{\lambda}{2} \implies \lambda = 2mg$$ ... ④

Now when the string is rotating, we have the situation shown in Figure 4.21.

Figure 4.21

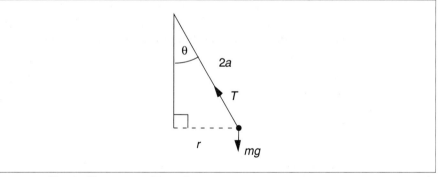

Vertically: $T \cos \theta - mg = 0$ ... ⑤

Horizontally: $T \sin \theta = \dfrac{mv^2}{r}$ ... ⑥

Δ : $\sin \theta = \dfrac{r}{2a}$ ... ⑦

Elasticity: $T = \dfrac{\lambda x}{a}$ ... ⑧

Since from ④, $\lambda = 2mg$ and we're told that the new length is $2a$, i.e. $x = a$, ⑧ becomes:

$$T = \frac{2mga}{a} = 2mg \qquad \dots ⑨$$

From ⑤ $T = \frac{mg}{\cos\theta} \Rightarrow \frac{mg}{\cos\theta} = 2mg \Rightarrow \cos\theta = \frac{1}{2}$

$$\Rightarrow \theta = 60°$$

From ⑥ $v^2 = \frac{T\sin\theta \times r}{m}$ and from ⑦, $r = 2a\sin\theta$, so

$$v^2 = \frac{T\sin\theta \times 2a\sin\theta}{m} \text{ and since } T = 2mg \text{ and } \sin\theta = \frac{\sqrt{3}}{2}$$

$$= 3ag \text{ then } v = \sqrt{3ag}$$

Here's another example, this time with the particle resting on a smooth table.

Example

A light elastic string, of natural length l and modulus $3mg$, has one end A attached to a fixed point O on a smooth horizontal table. A particle of mass m is attached to the other end of the string. The particle moves in a horizontal circle, centre O, so that the string rotates with constant angular velocity $\sqrt{\frac{2g}{l}}$. Find the radius of the circle.

The end A of the string is now raised vertically a distance $\frac{1}{2}l$ and held fixed. The particle P moves on the table in a circle, with OP having constant angular velocity $\sqrt{\frac{g}{l}}$. Show that the radius of the circle is $l\sqrt{2}$ and that the tension in the string is $\frac{3}{2}mg$. Find the magnitude of the reaction between the particle and the table.

Solution

Sometimes with these questions, you have to read carefully otherwise you might assume that, in the first part, the end of the string is *above* the table, which of course it isn't.

Figure 4.22

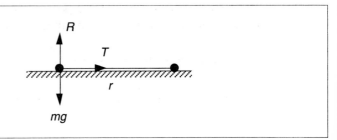

The force for the circular motion is coming entirely from the tension, and so with $\omega = \sqrt{\dfrac{2g}{l}}$

$$T = mr\omega^2 = mr\frac{2g}{l} \qquad \qquad \dots ①$$

Since the string is elastic, we have also that, with an extended length of r, i.e. extension $(r - l)$

$$T = \frac{\lambda x}{l} = \frac{3mg(r - l)}{l} \qquad \qquad \dots ②$$

Equating these two, $\qquad \dfrac{2mgr}{l} = \dfrac{3mg(r - l)}{l}$

$$2r = 3(r - l) = 3r - 3l$$
$$r = 3l$$

We need a new diagram for the next part.

Figure 4.23

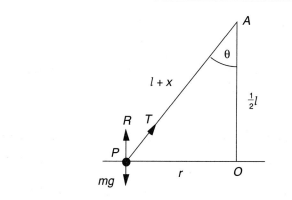

Vertically:	$T \cos \theta + R - mg = 0$	$\dots ③$
Horizontally:	$T \sin \theta = mr\omega^2$	$\dots ④$
Δ:	$\sin \theta = \dfrac{r}{l + x}$	$\dots ⑤$
Elasticity:	$T = \dfrac{\lambda x}{l}$	$\dots ⑥$

(We want to avoid using ③ if possible since it contains an R and at this stage we have no means of finding what this is or eliminating it.)

Since $\lambda = 3mg$, ⑥ becomes $T = \dfrac{3mgx}{l}$ and since $\sin \theta = \dfrac{r}{l + x}$

④ becomes $T \times \dfrac{r}{l + x} = mr\omega^2 \Rightarrow T = m\omega^2(l + x)$

Equating these two expressions for T,

$$\frac{3mgx}{l} = m\omega^2(l + x) \text{ and since } \omega^2 = \left(\sqrt{\frac{g}{l}}\right)^2 = \frac{g}{l}$$

$$\frac{3mgx}{l} = m\frac{g}{l}(l + x)$$

$$3x = l + x \Rightarrow 2x = l \Rightarrow x = \frac{l}{2}$$

From the right-angled Δ,

$$(l + x)^2 = \left(\tfrac{1}{2}l\right)^2 + r^2$$

$$\Rightarrow r^2 = \left(l + \frac{l}{2}\right)^2 - \left(\tfrac{1}{2}l\right)^2 = 2l^2 \Rightarrow r = l\sqrt{2}$$

Putting $x = \frac{l}{2}$ into ⑥, $\quad T = \dfrac{3mg \times \frac{1}{2}}{l} = \dfrac{3mg}{2}$

Now from ③ $\qquad R = mg - T\cos\theta$

$$= mg - \frac{3mg}{2} \times \frac{\frac{1}{2}l}{\frac{3}{2}l}$$

$$= mg - \frac{mg}{2} = \frac{mg}{2}$$

You should now be able to answer Exercises 13–14 on p. 71.

EXERCISES

1 Convert to rad s^{-1}:

(a) 1 rev s^{-1}

(b) 5π rev s^{-1}

2 Convert to rev s^{-1}:

(a) π rad s^{-1}

(b) 5 rad s^{-1}

3 Find the time for one revolution of a circle of 10 m when the particle is moving at:

(a) 4 rev s^{-1} (b) 3 rad s^{-1} (c) 4π rad s^{-1}

(d) 5 m s^{-1} (e) 7π m s^{-1}

4 A particle of mass 3 kg is moving in a horizontal circle under the action of a force of magnitude 4.8 N. If the speed of the particle is 4 m s^{-1}, find the radius of the circle.

5 Find the force necessary to keep a mass of 2 kg moving round a horizontal circle at the rate of 3 rev s^{-1} if the radius of the circle is 0.5 m.

6 A particle is attached to one end of a light string, the other end of which is fixed. When the particle moves in a horizontal circle with speed 2 m s^{-1} , the string makes an angle $\tan^{-1}\left(\frac{5}{12}\right)$ with the vertical. Show that the length of the string is approximately 2.5 m.

7 A particle P is attached to one end of a light inextensible string of length 0.125 m, the other end of the string being attached to a fixed point O. The particle describes with constant speed, and with the string taut, a horizontal circle whose centre is vertically below O. Given that the particle describes exactly two complete rev s^{-1} find, in terms of g and π, the cosine of the angle between OP and the vertical.

8 One end of a light inextensible string of length $5a$ is tied at a fixed point A which is at a distance $3a$ above a smooth horizontal table.
A particle of mass m, which is tied at the other end of the string, rotates with constant speed in a circle on the table. If the reaction between the particle and the table is R, find the tension in the string when:

(a) $R = 0$,

(b) $R = \dfrac{3mg}{4}$

Show that the respective times of one revolution for these two values of R are in the ratio 1: 2.

9 One end of a light inextensible string of length $8a$ is attached to the point A. The other end is attached to the point B vertically below A, where $AB = 4a$. A small smooth bead of mass m is threaded on the string and moves in a horizontal circle, with centre B and radius $3a$, with constant speed v. Find, in terms of m and g, the tension in the string and show that $v^2 = 6ga$.

10

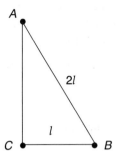

The ends of a light inextensible string *ABC* of length 3*l* are attached to fixed points *A* and *C*, *C* being vertically below *A* at a distance $l\sqrt{3}$ from *A*. At a distance 2*l* along the string from *A* a particle *B* of mass *m* is attached. When both portions of the string are taut, *B* is given a horizontal velocity *u*, and then continues to move in a circle with constant speed. Find the tensions in the two portions of the string and show that the motion is possible only if:

$$u^2 \geq \tfrac{1}{3}gl\sqrt{3}$$

11

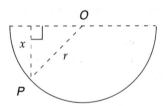

A particle *P* of mass *m* is moving in a horizontal circle with uniform speed *v* on the inner surface of a smooth fixed hemisphere which has centre *O* and radius *r*. If the verticle distance of *P* below the level of *O* is *x*, find expressions, in terms of *m*, *g*, *r* and *x* for *v* and for the reaction of the surface on *P*.

A light inextensible string is now attached to *P*. The string passes through a small hole at the lowest point of the hemisphere, and a particle of mass *m* hangs in equilibrium at the end of the string, so that the tension in the string is *mg*. Show that, if *P* moves on the surface in a horizontal circle with uniform speed *v* and with $x = \tfrac{1}{2}r$, then $v^2 = 3rg$.

12 A satellite S moves in a circular orbit about the centre O of the earth. The earth is to be assumed to be a sphere of radius R and the height of the satellite above the earth's surface is denoted by h. The acceleration due to gravity at a distance r from O is given by $\dfrac{k}{r^2}$ where k is a constant, and g is the value of this acceleration at the earth's surface. Assuming that the force of gravity acts along SO express k in terms of g and R and show that the angular speed of the satellite is:

$$\left(\frac{gR^2}{(R+h)^3} \right)^{\frac{1}{2}}$$

Given that $R = 6400$ km and $g = 9.8$ m s^{-2} find, to the nearest minute, the period of the satellite when its height above the earth is 1600 km and deduce that this period is approximately 2 hours.

13 An elastic string of length l and modulus $3mg$ has one end fixed to a point O. A particle of mass m is attached to the other end of the string and hangs in equilibrium. Find the stretched length of the string.

The particle is set in motion and describes a horizontal circle with constant angular speed ω. Given that the centre of the circle is at a distance l vertically below O, show

(a) that the stretched length of the string is $\dfrac{3l}{2}$

(b) that $\omega^2 l = g$.

(In this question take g to be 9.8 m s^{-2}.)

14 A light elastic string of natural length 0.2 m has one end attached to a fixed point O and a particle of mass 5 kg is attached to the other end.

When the particle hangs at rest, vertically below O, the string has length 0.225 m. Find the modulus of elasticity of the string.

The particle is made to describe a horizontal circle whose centre is vertically below O. The string remains taut throughout this motion and is inclined at an angle θ to the downward vertical through O.

(a) Given that the tension in the string is 98 N, find θ and the angular speed of the particle.

(b) Given that the string breaks when the tension in it exceeds 196 N, find the greatest angular speed which the particle can have without the string breaking.

SUMMARY

In this section we have been looking at the various situations which can involve uniform circular motion. You should now know:

- that there must be a force acting towards the centre of $mr\omega^2$ or $\dfrac{mv^2}{r}$

- the three main equations and use these to solve the system

- that the tension in a string with a threaded bead is the same throughout the string

- that the tensions in the two strings tied to a particle are not necessarily the same

- that for contact to be maintained with a surce, $R > 0$

- that for a string to remain taut, $T > 0$

- how to derive an additional equation relating the tension and extension when the string is elastic.

5

Simple harmonic motion

INTRODUCTION
In this section we are going to look at a particular type of system involving a variable force which is always directed towards a fixed point. As the particle moves away from this point, the force tending to pull it back increases until finally the particle stops its outward motion and starts moving towards the central point. On reaching this point, it continues past, whereupon the force pulls it back and so the process continues in an oscillation about this central point.

For your work on this section you will need to be familiar with the work on:

- variable acceleration from Module M1
- trigonometric equations, integration and differentiation from Modules P1 and P2.

What is simple harmonic motion?

When a particle is fastened to one end of an elastic string (the other end of which is fixed), it will rest in an equilibrium position when lowered slowly.

Figure 5.1

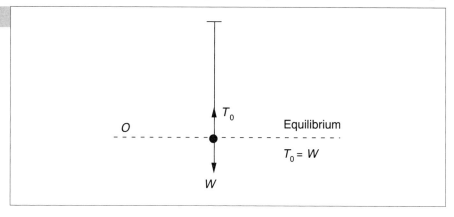

O

Equilibrium

T_0

$T_0 = W$

W

If the particle is moved away from this position, there will be a force acting which tends to bring it back. See Figure 5.2.

Figure 5.2

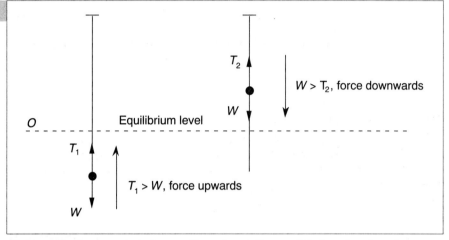

Taking displacements to be positive above the equilibrium level and negative below, we can see that the force is upwards (positive) when the displacement is negative and downwards (negative) when the displacement is positive. In fact, as we will show later, the force is directly proportional to the displacement away from the central point and since it has the opposite sign to the displacement , we can write

Force $= -kx$

where k is a positive constant and x is the displacement. Since force is mass $\times$ acceleration, we can use the form $\dfrac{d^2x}{dt^2}$ for the acceleration and write

$$-kx = m\,\frac{d^2x}{dt^2}$$

$$\Rightarrow \quad \frac{d^2x}{dt^2} = -\frac{k}{m}\,x$$

It turns out, since we shall be taking square roots later on, that the most convenient form for the constant $\dfrac{k}{m}$ is ω^2, and so we then have:

$$\frac{d^2x}{dt^2} = -\omega^2 x$$

This type of system, where the acceleration is directly proportional to the displacement but of the opposite sign, is called **simple harmonic motion.** Using the techniques from previous sections of systems with variable forces, we can find out some more about this motion.

Speed at any point

We shall return later to look at the case of a particle at the end of an elastic string, but for the moment we shall take a system where the particle oscillates about a central point O, reaching a maximum positive position of a and a minimum position of $-a$ relative to O. This maximum displacement a from the central point is called the **amplitude**.

The force acting on the particle is always **directed towards O**, the central point of the motion.

Let's have a look at the sign of the displacement, velocity and acceleration at various points in a cycle. Remember that velocities and accelerations are positive in the direction of x increasing and negative otherwise.

Figure 5.3

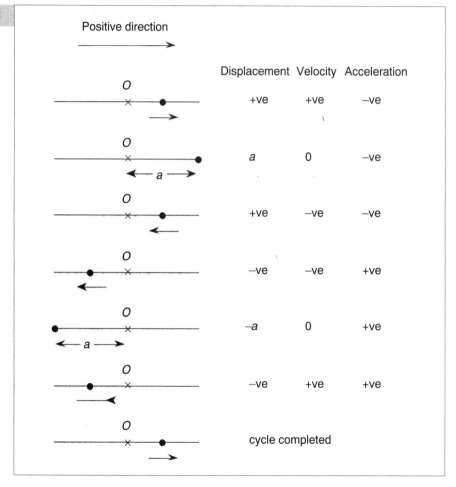

The acceleration, $-\omega^2 x$, involves displacement and so we use the form $v\dfrac{dv}{dx}$ and write:

$$v\dfrac{dv}{dx} = -\omega^2 x$$

i.e. $$\int v\,dv = \int -\omega^2 x\,dx$$

$$\Rightarrow \qquad \dfrac{v^2}{2} = -\omega^2\dfrac{x^2}{2} + C \qquad\qquad\qquad \dots \text{①}$$

For our pair of values of v and x, we know that the particle is temporarily at rest at the greatest positive distance, i.e. $x = a$. Putting these values into ①

$$0 = -\dfrac{\omega^2 a^2}{2} + C \implies C = \dfrac{\omega^2 a^2}{2} \qquad \text{and ① becomes}$$

$$\dfrac{v^2}{2} = \dfrac{-\omega^2 x^2}{2} + \dfrac{\omega^2 a^2}{2} \qquad\qquad \times \text{ by 2 and factorising,}$$

$$v^2 = \omega^2(a^2 - x^2)$$

From this equation, we can see that the maximum speed occurs when $x = 0$, i.e. the particle is at O, and then $v^2 = \omega^2 a^2$,

$$V_{max} = \omega a$$

Velocity and displacement at any time

If we take the positive square root of the equation

$$v^2 = \omega^2(a^2 - x^2)$$

we have $v = \omega\sqrt{a^2 - x^2}$

and writing v as $\dfrac{dx}{dt}$ we have the differential equation

$$\dfrac{dx}{dt} = \omega\sqrt{a^2 - x^2}$$

The solution of this is beyond the scope of our technique at the moment (it is covered in Module P3). We can show that it leads to:

$$\dfrac{x}{a} = \sin(\omega t + C)$$

$$x = a \sin (\omega t + C)$$

and differentiating, $\dfrac{dx}{dt} = a\omega \cos (\omega t + C)$

$$v = a\omega \cos (\omega t + C)$$

The value of the constant C depends on the position of the particle when $t = 0$. For convenience, we take this position either to be at 0, i.e. $x = 0$, or at the extreme positive point of the motion, i.e. $x = a$.

$x = 0$ when $t = 0$: Putting these values into $x = a \sin (\omega t + C)$ gives

$$0 = a \sin C \Rightarrow C = 0$$

and

$$x = a \sin \omega t, \quad v = a\omega \cos \omega t$$

Putting $x = a$ when $t = 0$ into $x = a \sin (\omega t + C)$ gives

$$a = a \sin C \qquad \Rightarrow \sin c = 1$$

$$\Rightarrow C = \frac{\pi}{2}$$

$$\text{and } x = a \sin \left(\omega t + \frac{\pi}{2} \right)$$

using formula for $\sin (A + B)$ $\quad = a \left[\sin \omega t \cos \dfrac{\pi}{2} + \cos \omega t \sin \dfrac{\pi}{2} \right]$

since $\sin \dfrac{\pi}{2} = 1$, $\cos \dfrac{\pi}{2} = 0$ $\qquad = a \cos \omega t$

$$x = a \cos \omega t, \quad v = -a\omega \sin \omega t$$

Time for a complete cycle

Both of the expressions for the distance involve periodic functions, sine and cosine, with a period of 2π. In the first expression, x will have the value of a when

$$a = a \sin \omega t \qquad \Rightarrow \sin \omega t = 1$$

$$\Rightarrow \omega t = \frac{\pi}{2}$$

This is the first positive solution, but there will be further solutions whenever $\sin \omega t$ has the value of 1, i.e. at $\dfrac{5\pi}{2}, \dfrac{9\pi}{2}, \dfrac{13\pi}{2}$ ... etc., where each solution is 2π more than the last.

The time T, called the **period** of the motion, between successive times at $x = a$ is given by $\omega T = 2\pi$

$$T = \frac{2\pi}{\omega}$$

It's important to know these equations – you will frequently find that you will be able to answer questions with just this knowledge and an ability to solve and rearrange. Let's collect them together and use them to solve a typical example.

$$\text{Acceleration} = \frac{d^2x}{dt^2} = -\omega^2 x$$

$$v^2 = \omega^2(a^2 - x^2), \quad a \text{ is amplitude}$$

$$v_{MAX} = \omega a$$

$$x = a \sin (\omega t + C)$$

$$v = a\omega \cos (\omega t + C)$$

$$T = \frac{2\pi}{\omega}$$

Example

A particle is describing simple harmonic motion in a straight line about a point O as centre. At a particular instant its displacement from O, its speed and the magnitude of its acceleration are 3 cm, 6 cm s^{-1} and 12 cm s^{-2} respectively.

Find:

(a) the greatest speed of the particle, and

(b) the period of its motion.

Solution

$x = 3$, $|v| = 6$ and $|$ acceleration $| = 12$

Since acceleration is $-\omega^2 x$, $|-\omega^2 x| = |-3\omega^2| = 3\omega^2 = 12$

i.e. $\omega^2 = 4$ and $\omega = 2$, since $\omega > 0$

$v^2 = \omega^2(a^2 - x^2) \Rightarrow 36 = 4(a^2 - 9)$

$\Rightarrow 9 = a^2 - 9 \Rightarrow a^2 = 18$

$\Rightarrow a = 3\sqrt{2}$, since $a > 0$

(a) $v_{MAX} = \omega a = 2 \times 3\sqrt{2} = 6\sqrt{2}$ cm s^{-1}

(b) $T = \dfrac{2\pi}{\omega} = \dfrac{2\pi}{2} = \pi$ seconds

---

Here's another slightly more involved example.

Example

A particle P of mass 8 kg describes simple harmonic motion with O as centre and has a speed of 6 m s^{-1} at a distance of 1 m from O and a speed of 2 m s^{-1} at a distance of 3 m from O.

(a) Find:

    (i) the amplitude of the motion

    (ii) the period of the motion

    (iii) the maximum speed of P

    (iv) the time taken to travel from O directly to one extreme point B of the motion.

(b) Determine the magnitude of:

    (i) the acceleration of P when at a distance of 2 m from O

    (ii) the force acting on P when at a distance of 2 m from O.

(c) Write down an expression for the displacement of P from O at any time t, given that P is at O at $t = 0$. Hence, or otherwise, find the time taken to travel directly from O to a point C between O and B and at a distance of 1 m from O. Find also the time taken to go directly from C to the point D between O and B and at a distance of 2 m from O.

Solution

(a) (i) We are going to use the equation $v^2 = \omega^2(a^2 - x^2)$ and substitute the pairs of values $\quad v = 6$ when $x = 1$

    and $\quad\quad\quad\quad\quad v = 2$ when $x = 3$

    First pair: $\quad 36 = \omega^2(a^2 - 1)$ ... ①

    Second pair: $\quad 4 = \omega^2(a^2 - 9)$ ... ②

$$① \div ② \text{ gives} \quad 9 = \frac{a^2 - 1}{a^2 - 9}$$

$$\Rightarrow \quad 9a^2 - 81 = a^2 - 1$$

$$8a^2 = 80$$

$$a^2 = 10 \quad \Rightarrow \quad a = \sqrt{10} \text{ m, the amplitude}$$

(ii) the period $T = \dfrac{2\pi}{\omega}$, so we need ω. Putting the value $a = \sqrt{10}$ into ①

gives $36 = \omega^2(10 - 1) \Rightarrow 9\omega^2 = 36$

$$\omega^2 = 4 \Rightarrow \quad \omega = 2 \quad \text{(taking positive value)}$$

The period T is then $\dfrac{2\pi}{\omega} = \dfrac{2\pi}{2} = \pi$ s

(iii) The maximum speed is given by $v_{\text{MAX}} = \omega a = 2\sqrt{10} \text{ m s}^{-1}$

(iv) The time for O to B is a quarter of the period, i.e. $\dfrac{\pi}{4}$ s.

(b) (i) Since the acceleration is $-\omega^2 x$, when $x = 2$ and $\omega = 2$, this will be -8, i.e. *magnitude* of 8 m s^{-2}

(ii) Force $F = \text{mass} \times \text{acceleration} \Rightarrow F = 8 \times 8 = 64 \text{ N}$

(c) When the motion starts at O, the central point, we use

$$x = a \sin \omega t, \quad v = a\omega \cos \omega t$$

Since $a = \sqrt{10}$ and $\omega = 2$, we have the distance x given by

$$x = \sqrt{10} \sin 2t$$

Time for O to C, $x = 1$

$$\Rightarrow \quad 1 = \sqrt{10} \sin 2t \quad \Rightarrow \quad \frac{1}{\sqrt{10}} = \sin 2t$$

$$\Rightarrow \quad t = 0.1609 \quad \text{(remember to use radians)}$$

Time for O to D, $x = 2$

$$\Rightarrow \quad 2 = \sqrt{10} \sin 2t \Rightarrow t = 0.3424$$

So time for C to D is the difference of these times,

i.e. $\quad 0.3424 - 0.1609 = 0.18$ s (2 d.p.)

You should now be able to answer Exercises 1–4 on pp. 87–88.

Tides

One naturally occurring example of simple harmonic motion (at least approximately) is the height of tidal water between the low and high tide marks. The centre of the motion will be the average of these heights. Here's an example of this.

Example

On a certain day the depth of water in a harbour entrance at low tide at 1200 hours is 5 m. At the following high tide at 1815 hours the depth of water is 15 m. In order to enter this harbour safely, a ship needs a minimum depth of 12 m of water. Given that the rise of the water level between low and high tides is simple harmonic, find:

(a) the earliest time during this tide at which the ship can safely enter the harbour

(b) the rate, in cm s^{-1}, at which the water level is rising at this earliest time.

Solution

The centre will be $\frac{5 + 15}{2}$ = 10 m depth, and so the amplitude, a, is $10 - 5 = 5$ m. Since half the period, from low to high tide, takes $6\frac{1}{4}$ hours, the period will be 12.5 hours,

i.e. $\quad \frac{2\pi}{\omega} = 12.5 \Rightarrow \omega = \frac{4\pi}{25}$

If we measure time from one of the extremes, low tide, we use the forms

$$x = a \cos \omega t \text{ and } v = -a\omega \sin \omega t$$

(a) We have to be careful with the signs – when $t = 0$, $x = -5$, i.e. 5 m below the central point so we need to put $a = -5$, giving $x = -5 \cos \omega t$. We need the time when the height is 12 m, i.e. 2 m above the central point. We find this from

$$2 = -5\cos \omega t \Rightarrow \frac{-2}{5} = \cos \omega t$$

and $\omega t = \cos^{-1}\left(\frac{-2}{5}\right) \Rightarrow t = \frac{1}{\omega}\cos^{-1}\left(\frac{-2}{5}\right) = \frac{25}{4\pi} \times (1.982)$ [in *radians*]

$$= 3.944 \text{ hours} = 3 \text{ hrs } 56.6 \text{ mins}$$

Since low tide is at 1200, the earliest time is 1557 (to nearest minute)

(b) At this time, using $v = 5\omega \sin \omega t$ and the fact that $\cos \omega t = -\frac{2}{5}$

$$\Rightarrow \sin \omega t = \sqrt{1 - \cos^2 \omega t} = \sqrt{1 - \frac{4}{25}} = \frac{\sqrt{21}}{5}$$

we have $v = 5 \times \frac{4\pi}{25} \times \frac{\sqrt{21}}{5} = 2.303 \text{ m h}^{-1} = 0.064 \text{ cm s}^{-1}$

Elastic strings

If a particle is suspended on an elastic string and disturbed from the equilibrium position it will perform simple harmonic motion provided that the string remains taut throughout. Let's have a look at a typical example of this idea.

Example

A light elastic string of natural length l has a particle of mass m attached at one end B and the other end A is fixed. If $AB = \frac{3l}{2}$ when the particle hangs freely at rest, show that the modulus of elasticity of the string is $2mg$.

When hanging at rest the particle is suddenly given a downward vertical velocity v so that it describes simple harmonic motion of amplitude $\frac{l}{2}$. Find, in terms of l and g, the period of this motion and the value of v.

Find the speed of the particle and the tension in the string when $AB = \frac{5l}{4}$.

Solution

The diagram represents the equilibrium position where $AB = \frac{3l}{2}$, so that the extension x in the elastic string is $\frac{l}{2}$

Figure 5.4

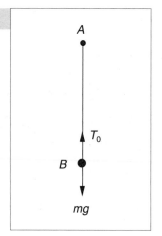

In equilibrium

$$T_0 = mg$$

and since $T = \frac{\lambda x}{l}$ and $x = \frac{l}{2}$,

$$\frac{\lambda x}{l} = mg \implies \frac{\lambda \frac{l}{2}}{l} = mg$$

$$\implies \lambda = 2mg$$

Now suppose that the elastic string is extended a further y from the equilibrium position, so that the tension is $\dfrac{\lambda \left(\frac{l}{2} + y \right)}{l}$.

Then the force acting on the particle is $T - mg$ upwards,

Figure 5.5

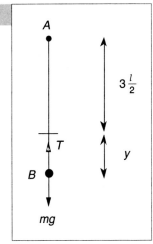

i.e. $\dfrac{\lambda\left(\frac{l}{2}+y\right)}{l} - mg$

$$= \dfrac{2mg\left(\frac{l}{2}+y\right)}{l} - mg$$

$$= \dfrac{mgl + 2mgy}{l} - mg$$

$$= mg + \dfrac{2mgy}{l} - mg$$

$$= \dfrac{2mgy}{l}$$

This is the **force** so the acceleration is $\dfrac{F}{m}$ i.e. $\dfrac{2gy}{l}$ **upwards**, i.e. opposite the direction in which y is increasing and so $-\dfrac{2gy}{l}$.

Since the acceleration in simple harmonic motion is $-\omega^2 y$, we have that

$$-\frac{2gy}{l} = -\omega^2 y \implies \omega^2 = \frac{2g}{l} \implies \omega = \sqrt{\frac{2g}{l}}$$

The period of the motion is $\dfrac{2\pi}{\omega} = 2\pi \times \sqrt{\dfrac{l}{2g}} = \pi\sqrt{\dfrac{2l}{g}}$

We're told that the amplitude of the motion is $\dfrac{l}{2}$, so $a = \dfrac{l}{2}$ and the maximum speed, $a\omega$, is $\dfrac{l}{2} \times \sqrt{\dfrac{2g}{l}} = \sqrt{\dfrac{gl}{2}}$. Since this maximum speed is the speed of the particle at O, this must be the **initial speed** of the particle, v.

When $AB = \dfrac{5l}{4}$, the particle is at the distance $x = l - \dfrac{5l}{4} = -\dfrac{l}{4}$ from the central point of the motion.

Using $v^2 = \omega^2(a^2 - x^2)$ where $\omega^2 = \dfrac{2g}{l}$ and $a^2 = \dfrac{l^2}{4}$,

$$v^2 = \frac{2g}{l}\left(\frac{l^2}{4} - \frac{l^2}{16}\right) = \frac{2g}{l}\left(\frac{3l^2}{16}\right) = \frac{3gl}{8}$$

and $v = \sqrt{\dfrac{3gl}{8}}$

The tension, with $x = \dfrac{l}{4}$ from the unstretched length and $\lambda = 2mg$, is

$$\frac{\lambda x}{l} = \frac{2\,mg}{l} \times \frac{l}{4} = \frac{mg}{2}$$

Simple pendulum

If the angle of displacement is relatively small, the motion of a simple pendulum is approximately simple harmonic. Let's look at an example of this to see how the defining equation is arrived at.

Example

The diagram shows a light rod of length l smoothly pivoted at one end O, and carrying a particle of mass m at its other end. The system hangs at rest under gravity, when at time $t = 0$ the particle is given a small horizontal speed u. At time t the angular displacement of the rod from the vertical is θ. Show that if θ is small, then approximately

$$\frac{d^2\theta}{dt^2} + \omega^2\theta = 0, \text{ where } \omega = \sqrt{\frac{g}{l}}$$

and deduce that the maximum value of θ is $\dfrac{u}{\sqrt{gl}}$.

Figure 5.6

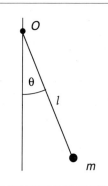

Solution   Look at Figure 5.7

Figure 5.7

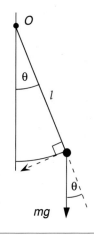

When the rod has been displaced to an angle θ, there is a restoring force of $mg \sin \theta$ perpendicular to the rod. Since when θ is small, $\sin \theta \approx \theta$

the force is $-mg \sin \theta \approx -mg \theta$.

This is the linear, tangential force, i.e. ma. We want to put it in terms of angular velocity, which we do by the relation $v = l\omega$, i.e. $v = l\dfrac{d\theta}{dt}$.

Differentiating both sides of this with respect to t gives $\dfrac{dv}{dt} = l\dfrac{d^2\theta}{dt^2}$.

Since $\dfrac{dv}{dt} = a$, and we have found that $ma \approx -mg\theta$

$$\Rightarrow \dfrac{dv}{dt} = l\dfrac{d^2\theta}{dt^2} \approx -g\theta$$

i.e. approximately, $l\dfrac{d^2\theta}{dt^2} = -g\theta \Rightarrow \dfrac{d^2\theta}{dt^2} + \dfrac{g}{l}\theta = 0$

i.e. $\dfrac{d^2\theta}{dt^2} + \omega^2\theta = 0$, where $\omega = \sqrt{\dfrac{g}{l}}$

This is the equation of simple harmonic motion. The maximum speed is at the centre of the motion, and we are told that the linear speed here is u. This implies that the maximum angular velocity, $\dfrac{d\theta}{dt}$, is $\dfrac{u}{l}$ (using $v = l\omega$). Since the maximum velocity in simple harmonic motion is amplitude $\times \omega$, we have amplitude is

$$\dfrac{1}{\omega} \times \dfrac{u}{l} = \dfrac{u}{l}\sqrt{\dfrac{l}{g}}$$

i.e. the amplitude, maximum θ is $\dfrac{u}{\sqrt{gl}}$

Other applications

Here is an example where we model the movement of a planet around its star using SHM.

Example   An astronomer observes a faint object close to a star. Continued observations show the object apparently moving in a straight line through the star as shown in the diagram.

Figure 5.8

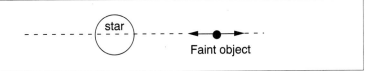

The astronomer is able to estimate the apparent distance of the object from the star and records this at 30-day intervals, resulting in the following table.

Day	t	0	30	60	90	120
Distance (10^{11}) m	x	1.0	1.5	1.9	2.0	1.9

The apparent movement of the object relative to the star is to be modelled by the simple harmonic motion equation:

$$x = 2 \sin (\omega t + \varepsilon)$$

where x is the apparent distance of the object from the star, t is the time in days since the recordings started and ω and ε are constants to be determined.

(a) Use the values of x for $t = 0$ and $t = 90$ to find values for the constants ω and ε. Verify that the other values for x are consistent with this model.

The astronomer believes that the object is a planet in a circular orbit about the star and that it is being observed from the plane of its orbit. Assuming that this is the case, find:

(b) the radius of the planet's orbit

(c) the linear speed in orbit of the planet in m s^{-1}

(d) the number of Earth days the planet takes to go round its star.

Solution

(a) Substituting the values $x = 1$ when $t = 0$ into the given modelling equation,

$$1 = 2 \sin (0 + \varepsilon) \quad \Rightarrow \sin \varepsilon = \frac{1}{2} \Rightarrow \varepsilon = \frac{\pi}{6}$$

$$x = 2 \text{ when } t = 90 \Rightarrow 2 = 2 \sin \left(90\omega + \frac{\pi}{6} \right)$$

$$\Rightarrow \quad \sin \left(90\omega + \frac{\pi}{6} \right) = 1$$

$$\Rightarrow \quad 90\omega + \frac{\pi}{6} = \frac{\pi}{2} \Rightarrow 90\omega = \frac{\pi}{3} \Rightarrow \omega = \frac{\pi}{270}$$

This gives the equation as $x = 2 \sin \left(\dfrac{\pi t}{270} + \dfrac{\pi}{6} \right)$ ...①

You can check that this equation gives the required distances, e.g. when $t = 30$

$$x = 2 \sin \left(\frac{\pi t}{270} \times 30 + \frac{\pi}{6} \right)$$

$$= 2 \sin \left(\frac{5\pi}{18} \right) = 1.5 \text{ (1 d.p.)}$$

(b) Since the maximum value of x from equation ① is 2 and the minimum is –2, the amplitude of the motion is 2×10^{11} m, which is the radius of the planet's orbit.

(c) Since $v = rw$, linear speed is

$$2 \times 10^{11} \times \frac{\pi}{270} = 2.327 \times 10^9 \text{ m/day}$$

$$= \frac{2.327 \times 10^9}{24 \times 3600} = 2.69 \times 10^4 \text{ m s}^{-1}$$

(d) We know that $x = 2$ when $t = 90$. The next time that x is 2 is when

$$\frac{\pi t}{270} + \frac{\pi}{6} = \frac{\pi}{2} + 2\pi$$

$$\Rightarrow \quad \frac{\pi t}{270} = \frac{7\pi}{3} \quad \Rightarrow t = 630$$

The difference between these is 540 days, the period of rotation.

You should now be able to answer Exercises 5–11 on pp. 88–89.

EXERCISES

1 A particle P describes simple harmonic oscillations of amplitude 7 cm and period 4 s. Find the maximum speed of P and its speed when at a distance of 3 cm from the centre of oscillation.

2 A particle moves with simple harmonic motion along a straight line. At a certain instant it is 9 m away from the centre O of its motion and has a speed of 6 m s^{-1} and an acceleration of $\frac{9}{4}$ m s^{-2}. Find:

(a) the period of the motion
(b) the amplitude of the motion
(c) the greatest speed of the particle.

3 (a) A particle of mass 0.2 kg is performing 5 complete oscillations per second in simple harmonic motion between A and B, where AB is 0.1 m.
Find the maximum speed of the particle and the greatest force exerted on it.

(b) While at A the particle is struck a blow in the direction BA to double the amplitude without altering the frequency. Show that the speed of the particle immediately after the blow is approximately 2.7 m s^{-1}.

4 A particle is moving with simple harmonic motion in a straight line between the extreme points A and B; O is the centre of the oscillations. When the particle is 4 m from O, its speed is 4 m s^{-1}, and when the particle is 2 m from O, its speed is 8 m s^{-1}. Calculate the distance AB and the time taken by the particle for one oscillation.

If the particle is of mass 2 kg, find its kinetic energy when it is 2 m from A.

Find the time taken by the particle to travel directly from A to M, where M is the mid-point of OB.

5 A particle of mass 2 kg is acted upon by a variable force which makes it move in simple harmonic motion about O on the straight line Ox. Given that the maximum speed attained is 0.5 m s^{-1} and the maximum acceleration is 0.1 m s^{-2}, find the period of the motion. Show that the amplitude of the motion is 2.5 m.

6 A particle P performs simple harmonic oscillations of amplitude 4 cm and period 8 s.

Find:

(a) the maximum speed of P

(b) the maximum magnitude of the acceleration of P

(c) the speed of P when it is 2 cm from the centre of the oscillations.

7 A particle of mass m is suspended from a fixed point O by a light elastic string of natural length l and modulus λ. When the mass is hanging freely at rest the extension of the string is a. Find λ in terms of m, g, l and a.

Suppose that the particle is pulled down a small vertical distance from its equilibrium position and then released from rest. Show that its subsequent motion is simple harmonic with period

$$2\pi\sqrt{\frac{a}{g}}$$

8 A particle moves along the x-axis and describes simple harmonic motion of period 16 s about the origin O as centre. At time $t = 4$ s, $x = 12$ cm and the particle is moving towards O with speed $\frac{5\pi}{8}$ cm s^{-1}.

Given that the displacement, x, at any time t may be written as

$$x = a \cos(\omega t + \phi),$$

find a, ω and ϕ.

9 A particle of mass 4 kg executes simple harmonic motion with amplitude 2 m and period 10 s. The particle starts from rest at time $t = 0$. Find its maximum speed and the time at which half the maximum speed is first attained. Find also the maximum value of the magnitude of the force required to maintain the motion.
(You may leave your answers in terms of π.)

[Standard formulae relating to simple harmonic motion may be quoted without proof.]

10 In a certain tidal estuary the water level rises and falls with simple harmonic motion. On a particular day a marker indicates that the depths of water at low and high tides are 4 m and 10 m and that these occur at 1100 and 1720 respectively.

Calculate:

(a) the speed, in m h^{-1}, at which the water level is rising at 1235

(b) the time, during this tide, at which the depth of water is $8\frac{1}{2}$ m.

11 (a) The natural length and modulus of a light elastic spring AB are l_0 m and λ N respectively. The end A of the spring is fixed. When a particle of mass M kg is attached to the spring at B and hangs freely under gravity, the extension of the spring is 0.2 m. The mass is pulled down through a further small distance so that the spring is extended, and then released from rest. Show that the subsequent motion is simple harmonic of period $\frac{2\pi}{7}$ s.

(b) A particle moves with simple harmonic motion along the x-axis about the origin O, of period $\frac{2\pi}{\omega}$ and amplitude a.

(i) Write down expressions giving the acceleration and speed at a point distance x from O. At a certain time, $x = 3$ m and the speed and the acceleration of the particle are equal in magnitude. Given further that the maximum speed in the motion is 2 m s^{-1}, show that the period and amplitude of the motion are $2\sqrt{3}\,\pi$ s and $2\sqrt{3}$ m respectively.

(ii) Two particles A and B move in simple harmonic motion about O with amplitude $2\sqrt{3}$ m and period $2\sqrt{3}\,\pi$ s. A is released from rest at time $t = 0$ from the extreme point P where $x = 2\sqrt{3}$. Particle B is released from P at time $t = \frac{\sqrt{3}}{2}\pi$ s.

Show that the particles will collide $\frac{3\sqrt{3}}{4}\pi$ s after the release of B.

Find how far from O the collision will occur.

SUMMARY   This section has covered the principles of simple harmonic motion. You should now know all the standard formulae for simple harmonic motion and be able to apply them to mathematical problems including those involving tides, particles connected to an elastic string or spring or simple pendulums. To summarise these equations:

- Acceleration is $\dfrac{d^2x}{dt^2} = -\omega^2 x$
- $v^2 = \omega^2(a^2 - x^2)$, a is amplitude
- $v_{MAX} = \omega a$
- $x = a \sin(\omega t + C)$
- $v = a\omega \cos(\omega t + C)$
- $T = \dfrac{2\pi}{\omega}$

You should also know that:

- the greatest speed is reached as the particle passes the central point of the motion
- the greatest force (and so acceleration) is exerted at the extreme displacements of the particle
- a quick diagram showing the positions indicated in the question can help avoid misunderstanding.

Conservation of energy

INTRODUCTION We have already used the principle of conservation of mechanical energy when we looked at dynamic systems involving elastic strings or springs. We are now going to look at some different applications of this principle – for systems where a particle is describing a vertical circle.

You will be using some of the material found in the sections on:
- circular motion
- work, energy and power.

Motion in a vertical circle

We have looked at different systems of an object moving in a **horizontal** circle. In this section we're going to look at the motion of a particle which moves in a **vertical** circle and the conditions which are necessary for this motion to be possible.

Basic equations

There are two main ways of looking at the system and both give an equation – from these two equations we can generally solve the motion. The two ways are:

(a) conservation of energy
(b) circular motion.

From (a) we know that the sum of the kinetic and potential energies at any point is constant, so we have an equation linking velocities and position.

From (b) we know that there must be a force with a component of $\dfrac{mv^2}{r}$ acting towards the centre and so we obtain an equation which links the velocity to a force, usually a tension if on a string or a normal reaction.

We can apply this pair of determining equations to a number of situations: where the particle is:

- suspended at the end of a fixed inelastic string
- threaded on a smooth hoop
- on the inner surface of a spherical or cylindrical shell
- on the outer surface of a sphere or cylinder.

In all cases the analysis is very similar and even identical except that a different letter appears in the equations.

Before we start a detailed analysis we'll have a look at different types of motion dependent upon the initial conditions.

Initial velocity

The initial velocity given to the particle is important since it determines the kind of path taken subsequently. If we look at the case of a particle inside a cylindrical shell we can distinguish three different cases. We are assuming that the particle starts from the bottom of the shell.

Figure 6.1

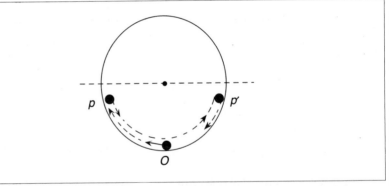

Low initial velocity: the particle reaches a point p below the level of the centre of the circle, stops, returns to O and continues to a corresponding point p' on the opposite side of the circle. With no friction, this will continue indefinitely.

Figure 6.2

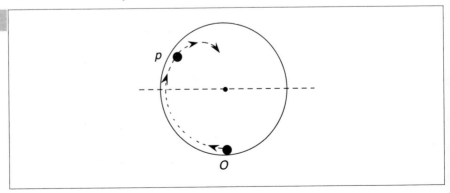

Medium initial velocity: the particle reaches a point *p* above the level of the centre and then loses contact with the surface. It continues as a projectile.

Figure 6.3

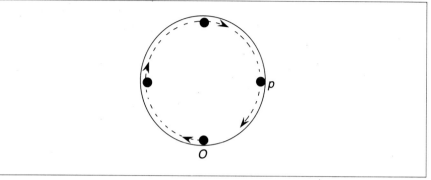

High initial velocity: the particle reaches the top of the circle still in contact with the surface. It continues indefinitely describing complete circles if there is no friction.

We'll have a look now at the way in which the two equations allow us to find the precise conditions corresponding to the different types of motion.

Example A particle *P* of mass *m* is attached to one end of a light inextensible string of length *a*. The other end of the string is attached to a fixed point *O*. When *P* is at rest vertically below *O*, it is given a horizontal speed *u*.

(a)   Find the tension in the string when *OP* makes an angle θ with the *upward* vertical

(b)   Hence, show that *P* will leave its circular path if $2ga < u^2 < 5ga$.

Solution Figure 6.4 represents the initial position of the particle and the subsequent position when *OP* makes an angle θ with the upward vertical, *P* being at a vertical height *h* above the initial position.

Figure 6.4

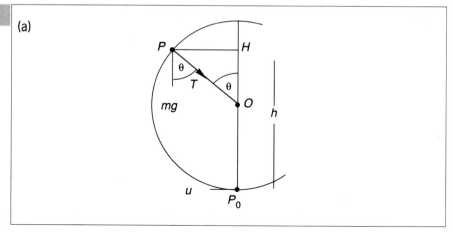

We'll find our equations from our two sources.

(a) *Conservation of energy*: If we take the zero potential level to be at the initial position, the initial sum of the energies is

$$\tfrac{1}{2}mu^2 + O = \tfrac{1}{2}mu^2 \qquad\qquad\qquad \dots \text{①}$$

   KE   KE

At the later position, if we call the velocity v, the kinetic energy will be $\tfrac{1}{2}mv^2$ and we need to find its potential energy, mgh. From $\triangle OPH$,

$$\cos\theta = \frac{OH}{OP} \Rightarrow OH = OP\cos\theta = a\cos\theta$$

$$h = P_0O + OH = a + a\cos\theta = a(1 + \cos\theta)$$

giving a potential energy of $mga\,(1 + \cos\theta)$

This gives the new sum of energies

$$\tfrac{1}{2}mv^2 + mga\,(1 + \cos\theta) \qquad\qquad\qquad \dots \text{②}$$

and equating these sums ① and ② by conservation of energy,

$$\tfrac{1}{2}mu^2 = \tfrac{1}{2}mv^2 + mga\,(1 + \cos\theta) \qquad\qquad \dots \text{③}$$

Circular motion: Since the motion is circular, we know the force towards the centre must be $\dfrac{mv^2}{a}$. Resolving the weight along PO together with the tension gives

$$mg\cos\theta + T = \frac{mv^2}{a} \qquad\qquad\qquad \dots \text{④}$$

Rearranging $\qquad\qquad T = \dfrac{mv^2}{a} - mg\cos\theta \qquad\qquad \dots \text{⑤}$

But from ③, $\qquad \tfrac{1}{2}mv^2 = \tfrac{1}{2}mu^2 - mga\,(1 + \cos\theta)$

$\times \dfrac{2}{a} \qquad\qquad\qquad \dfrac{mv^2}{a} = \dfrac{mu^2}{a} - 2mg\,(1 + \cos\theta)$

This into ⑤ gives $\qquad T = \dfrac{mu^2}{a} - 2mg\,(1 + \cos\theta) - mg\cos\theta$

$$= \frac{mu^2}{a} - 2mg - 2\,mg\cos\theta - mg\cos\theta$$

i.e. $\quad T = \dfrac{mu^2}{a} - mg\,(2 + 3\cos\theta) \qquad\qquad \dots \text{⑥}$

(b) The question is asking for the range of values of u which correspond to the second of the three possible cases, i.e. where the string becomes slack ($T = 0$) and the particle continues as a projectile.

Putting $T = 0$ into ⑥ gives

$$\frac{mu^2}{a} = mg\,(2 + 3\cos\theta)$$

$$\Rightarrow \frac{u^2}{ga} = 2 + 3\cos\theta \Rightarrow \cos\theta = \frac{1}{3}\left(\frac{u^2}{ga} - 2\right) \qquad \ldots⑦$$

Since the particle is above the level of the centre of the circle, $0 < \theta < \dfrac{\pi}{2}$ and so $0 < \cos\theta < 1$

i.e. $\quad 0 < \dfrac{1}{3}\left(\dfrac{u^2}{ga} - 2\right) < 1 \ $ from ⑦

$$\Rightarrow \quad 0 < \frac{u^2}{ga} - 2 < 3$$

$$\Rightarrow \quad 2 < \frac{u^2}{ga} < 5$$

$$\Rightarrow \quad 2ga < u^2 < 5ga$$

Maximum and minimum tensions

At the bottom of the circle, the velocity of the particle is greatest

Figure 6.5

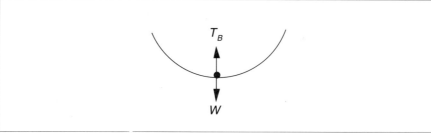

$$T_B - W + \frac{mv_B^2}{a} \Rightarrow T_B = \frac{mv_B^2}{a} + W \qquad \ldots Ⓐ$$

and at the top, the velocity is least

Figure 6.6

$$T_T + W = \frac{mv_T^2}{a} \Rightarrow T_T = \frac{mv_T^2}{a} - W \qquad \ldots Ⓑ$$

and you can see by comparing the expressions Ⓐ and Ⓑ for the tensions at the top and bottom that the greatest tension corresponds to the greatest velocity, at the bottom, and similarly the least tension with the least velocity at the top.

Here's an example of this.

Example	A particle P, of mass m, is attached to a fixed point O by a light inextensible string of length a, and is executing complete circular revolutions in a vertical plane. When OP is inclined at an angle θ to the downward vertical, the tension T in the string is given by

$$T = mg\,(3\cos\theta - 2) + \frac{mu^2}{a}$$

where u is the speed of P when it passes through its lowest points. Show that, if $3T_0$ and T_0 are the greatest and least tensions in the string during the motion, then

$$u^2 = 8ag \text{ and } T = T_0\,(2 + \cos\theta).$$

Solution	The minimum tension is when $\theta = 180°$, giving

$$T_0 = mg\,(3\cos 180° - 2) + \frac{mu^2}{a} = \frac{mu^2}{a} - 5\,mg \qquad \dots ①$$

The maximum tension is when $\theta = 0°$, which gives

$$3T_0 = mg\,(3\cos 0° - 2) + \frac{mu^2}{a} = \frac{mu^2}{a} + mg \qquad \dots ②$$

Putting ① into ②, $3\left(\dfrac{mu^2}{a} - 5\,mg\right) = \dfrac{mu^2}{a} + mg$

$$\frac{3mu^2}{a} - 15mg = \frac{mu^2}{a} + mg$$

$$\frac{2mu^2}{a} = 16mg \quad \Rightarrow u^2 = 8ag$$

This into ① gives $T_0 = \dfrac{8mag}{a} - 5\,mg = 3mg \qquad \dots ③$

and from the given equation,

$$T = mg\,(3\cos\theta - 2) + \frac{8mag}{a}$$

$$= 3mg\cos\theta - 2mg + 8mg$$

$$= 3mg\cos\theta + 6mg = 3mg\,(2 + \cos\theta)$$

$$= T_0\,(2 + \cos\theta) \text{ from } ③$$

Threaded particle

When the particle is threaded on something like a smooth hoop which keeps the motion circular, slightly different equations arise. This is because the reaction of the hoop on the particle can act *towards* or *away from* the centre of the motion. Let's look at the case where the particle is moving on the upper half of the vertical circle.

Figure 6.7

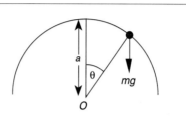

Here we can see that the weight has a component $mg \cos \theta$ *towards* the centre. When the velocity is large, this central component may be insufficient for the force needed inwards, i.e. $\dfrac{mv^2}{a}$. In this case the additional force is supplied by the reaction which then also acts inwards. When the velocity is not so large, the inward component of the weight may be enough, or more than enough, to supply the necessary force inwards and the reaction will act away from the centre. Here is an example of this.

Example

A small bead of mass m slides on a smooth circular hoop, with centre O and radius a, which is fixed in a vertical plane. The bead is projected with speed u, where $2ag < u^2 < 4ag$, from A, the lowest point of the hoop, and at subsequent time t, the bead is at a point P where angle $POA = \theta$. Find in terms of u, a, g and θ, an expression for $\left(\dfrac{d\theta}{dt}\right)^2$ and deduce that R, the magnitude of the force exerted by the hoop on the bead, is given by

$$aR = \left| mu^2 - mga\,(2 - 3\cos\theta) \right|.$$

Solution Figure 6.8 shows this system.

Figure 6.8

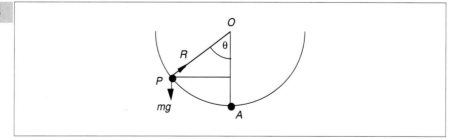

By energy, $\frac{1}{2} mu^2 = \frac{1}{2} mv^2 + mga\,(1 - \cos\theta)$

$\Rightarrow \qquad v^2 = u^2 - 2ga\,(1 - \cos\theta)$ \hfill ...①

Since $v = a\omega = a\left(\dfrac{d\theta}{dt}\right)$,

$$v^2 = a^2\left(\frac{d\theta}{dt}\right)^2$$

$\Rightarrow \qquad \left(\dfrac{d\theta}{dt}\right)^2 = \dfrac{1}{a^2}\left[u^2 - 2ga\,(1 - \cos\theta)\,\right]$

Inward force $R_1 - mg\cos\theta = ma\left(\dfrac{d\theta}{dt}\right)^2$

$$= \frac{m}{a}\left[u^2 - 2ga\,(1 - \cos\theta)\,\right]$$

$$= \frac{mu^2}{a} - 2mg + 2mg\,\cos\theta$$

$\Rightarrow \qquad R_1 = \dfrac{mu^2}{a} - 2mg + 3mg\,\cos\theta$

$\Rightarrow \qquad aR_1 = mu^2 - mga\,(2 - 3\cos\theta)$

Depending on the initial value of u^2, R_1 can be positive or negative for different values of θ, and we put

$$aR = \left|\, mu^2 - mga\,(2 - 3\cos\theta)\,\right| \quad \text{where } R = |R_1|$$

Here's another example of vertical circles at the end of a string where the conditions also change during the motion – this time the string meets a peg at its mid-point.

| **Example** | The end O of a light inelastic string OP of length a is fixed and a particle of mass m is attached at the other end P. The particle is held with the string taut and horizontal and is given a velocity u vertically downwards. When the string becomes vertical it begins to wrap itself around a small smooth peg, A, at a depth $\dfrac{a}{2}$ below O. Find the tension in the string when AP subsequently makes an angle θ with the downward vertical and show that if $u = 0$ the string becomes slack when $\cos\theta = -\dfrac{2}{3}$. |

Find the minimum value of u in order that the particle makes complete revolutions about A.

Solution

In Figure 6.9 the path of the particle is represented as it starts on the right and moves clockwise until the string is vertical. It then begins to wrap itself around the peg and P_1 represents the position when the string makes an angle θ with the downward vertical.

Figure 6.9

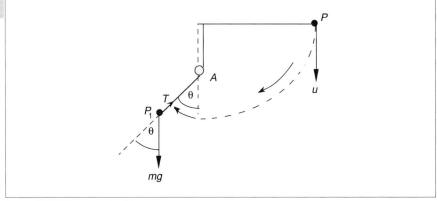

If we take the zero potential level to be the bottom of the circle, then the sum of the kinetic and potential energies in the initial position with the string horizontal will be

$$\frac{1}{2} mu^2 + mga \qquad \qquad \dots ①$$

$\qquad$ KE $\qquad$ KE

Looking at the vertical position of P_1 more closely

Figure 6.10

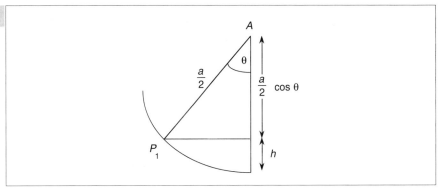

we can see that the height h will be $\dfrac{a}{2} - \dfrac{a}{2} \cos \theta$ and if we call the velocity of the particle at this point v, the sum of the energies at P_1 will be

$$\frac{1}{2} mv^2 + mg \left(\frac{a}{2} - \frac{a}{2} \cos \theta \right) \qquad \qquad \dots ②$$

Equating these two expressions for the total energy,

$$\frac{1}{2}mu^2 + mga = \frac{1}{2}mv^2 + mg\left(\frac{a}{2} - \frac{a}{2}\cos\theta\right)$$

$$= \frac{1}{2}mv^2 + \frac{mga}{2} - \frac{mga}{2}\cos\theta$$

i.e. $\frac{1}{2}mv^2 = \frac{1}{2}mu^2 + \frac{1}{2}mga + \frac{1}{2}mga\cos\theta$

$\times \frac{2}{m}$ $v^2 = u^2 + ag(1 + \cos\theta)$ ... ①

Now since the motion around the peg is circular with radius $\frac{a}{2}$, the force

towards the centre, i.e. the peg, must be $\dfrac{mv^2}{\left(\frac{a}{2}\right)}$

i.e. $T - mg\cos\theta = \dfrac{2mv^2}{a}$ ... ②

Putting ① into this equation,

$$T = \frac{2m[u^2 + ag(1 + \cos\theta)]}{a} + mg\cos\theta$$

$$= \frac{2mu^2}{a} + 2mg(1 + \cos\theta) + mg\cos\theta$$

$$= \frac{2mu^2}{a} + mg(2 + 3\cos\theta)$$ ... ③

If $u = 0$ and $T = 0$ when the string becomes slack

$$0 = mg(2 + 3\cos\theta) \Rightarrow \cos\theta = -\frac{2}{3}$$

Since we need $T \geq 0$ at the top, where $\theta = 180°$, putting these values into ③, the condition for complete circles becomes

$$\frac{2mu^2}{a} + mg(2 + 3\cos 180°) \geq 0 \quad \text{and since } \cos 180° = -1$$

$$\frac{2mu^2}{a} + mg(2 - 3) \geq 0 \quad \Rightarrow \frac{2mu^2}{a} \geq mg$$

$$\Rightarrow u^2 \geq \frac{ag}{2} \text{ or } u \geq \sqrt{\frac{ag}{2}}$$

Motion inside a smooth sphere

Here we have a normal reaction taking the place of the tension in the previous case – otherwise the equations are identical.

Figure 6.11

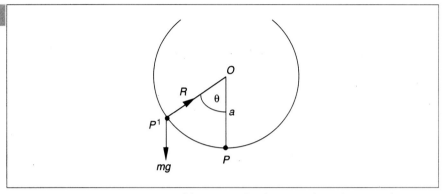

Suppose we are given an initial horizontal velocity, when the particle is at P, of $\sqrt{\dfrac{7ag}{2}}$

The **minimum** horizontal velocity for complete circles is the same as before, i.e. $\sqrt{5ag}$ and since $\sqrt{\dfrac{7ag}{2}}$ is less than this, the particle will leave the surface of the sphere. To find out the angle θ when this happens, we use the same equation as for a complete circle, with R instead of T, i.e.

$$R = \frac{mu^2}{a} + mg(3\cos\theta - 2) \qquad \ldots \text{①}$$

Now we're told that $u = \sqrt{\dfrac{7ag}{2}}$ and we want the point at which the particle loses contact with the sphere, i.e. $R = 0$. Putting these values into ①,

$$0 = \frac{m}{a}\left(\frac{7ag}{2}\right) + mg(3\cos\theta - 2)$$

$$= \frac{7mg}{2} + 3mg\cos\theta - 2mg$$

$$\Rightarrow 3mg\cos\theta = -\frac{3}{2}mg$$

i.e. $\cos\theta = -\dfrac{1}{2} \Rightarrow \theta = 120°$

and the line joining the particle at this point, i.e. OQ, makes an angle of $180° - 120° = 60°$ with the **upward** vertical.

Figure 6.12

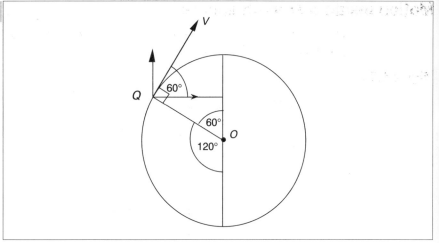

We want to find the velocity at this point – we can use equation ⑤ for a complete circle i.e.

$$mv^2 = mu^2 - 2mga\,(1 - \cos\theta)$$

Substituting

$$u = \sqrt{\frac{7ag}{2}} \text{ and } \cos\theta = -\frac{1}{2} \text{ gives}$$

$$mv^2 = m\left(\frac{7ag}{2}\right) - 2mga\left(\frac{3}{2}\right) = \frac{mga}{2}$$

i.e. $v^2 = \dfrac{ag}{2} \Rightarrow v = \sqrt{\dfrac{ag}{2}}$

The **vertical** component of this velocity (see Figure 6.12) will be $v\sin 60°$,

i.e. $\sqrt{\dfrac{ag}{2}} \times \dfrac{\sqrt{3}}{2} = \dfrac{1}{2}\sqrt{\dfrac{3ag}{2}}$

If H is the greatest height above Q, we have

$$u = \frac{1}{2}\sqrt{\frac{3ag}{2}}, v = 0, s = H, a = -g$$

$$\Rightarrow \qquad v^2 = u^2 + 2as$$

$$\Rightarrow \qquad 0 = \frac{1}{4} \times \frac{3ag}{2} - 2gH$$

$$\Rightarrow \qquad 2gH = \frac{3ag}{8} \qquad \Rightarrow H = \frac{3a}{16}$$

Since Q is at a height $a + a \cos 60°$ above O, i.e. $\dfrac{3a}{2}$, the greatest height above

O reached by the particle is $\dfrac{3a}{2} + \dfrac{3a}{16} = \dfrac{27a}{16}$

Motion on the outer surface of a sphere

The two main equations in this case still come from conservation of energy and circular motion, although the last of these takes a slightly different form.

Figure 6.13

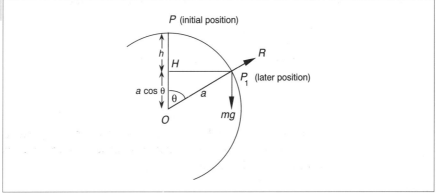

If the particle starts from rest, as it usually does in questions of this kind, and we take the top of the circle to be the zero potential level, then the sum of the energies at P_1 is zero.

When the particle is at P_1, where OP_1 makes an angle θ with OP, if we assume the velocity to be v then the kinetic energy will be $\frac{1}{2}mv^2$.

From the triangle OHP_1, $OH = a \cos \theta$ and so h, the vertical distance fallen, will be $a - a \cos \theta$ and the potential energy $mg(a - a \cos \theta)$.

At P_1 then,

$$\frac{1}{2}mv^2 - mg\,(a - a \cos \theta) = 0$$

$$\Rightarrow \frac{1}{2}mv^2 = mg(a - a \cos \theta)$$

$$v^2 = 2ag(1 - \cos \theta) \qquad\qquad \text{...①}$$

Since the motion is circular, the force towards the centre is $\dfrac{mv^2}{a}$,

i.e. $mg \cos \theta - R = \dfrac{mv^2}{a}$ \qquad\qquad ...②

Substituting ① into ②,

$$mg \cos \theta - R = \frac{m}{a} \times 2ag(1 - \cos \theta)$$

$$= 2mg - 2mg \cos \theta$$

then $\quad R = 3mg \cos \theta - 2mg$

$$= mg(3 \cos \theta - 2) \qquad \qquad \ldots ③$$

The condition for the particle to be in contact with the sphere is $R > 0$,

i.e. $\quad mg(3 \cos \theta - 2) > 0$

$$\cos \theta > \frac{2}{3}$$

It loses contact, i.e. $R = 0$, at the point where $\cos \theta = \frac{2}{3}$

Putting these values into ②,

$$mg \times \frac{2}{3} - 0 = \frac{mv^2}{a} \quad \Rightarrow v^2 = \frac{2ag}{3}$$

and $\quad v = \sqrt{\dfrac{2ag}{3}}$

If you are asked about the **subsequent** motion of the particle, it will be a projectile whose initial horizontal and vertical components come from the value of v and θ at this point.

Figure 6.14

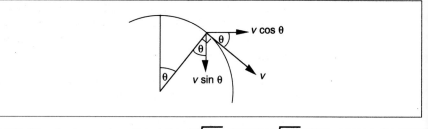

Horizontally $\quad u_H \quad = v \cos \theta = \sqrt{\dfrac{2ag}{3}} \times \dfrac{2}{3} = \dfrac{2}{3} \sqrt{\dfrac{2ag}{3}}$

Vertically $\quad u_V \quad = v \sin \theta$

$$= \sqrt{\dfrac{2ag}{3}} \times \dfrac{\sqrt{5}}{3}$$

$$= \dfrac{1}{3} \sqrt{\dfrac{10ag}{3}}$$

That concludes the section on vertical circles. You should now be able to answer Exercises 1–6 on pp. 105–106.

EXERCISES

1 One end of a light inextensible string of length a is fixed at a point O and to the other end P is attached a particle of mass m. The string is held taut with OP horizontal and the particle is given a vertical velocity V. Find the least value of V in order that the particle describes complete circles.

If the string breaks when the tension in the string is $\frac{15}{2} mg$, find:

(a) the angle OP makes with the vertical when the string breaks if $V = \sqrt{6ag}$

(b) the minimum value of V for the string to break.

2 A particle of mass m is attached to the end A of a light inextensible string OA of length a. The other end O of the string is fixed. Initially A is held vertically above O with the string taut and the particle is projected horizontally with speed V, where $V > \sqrt{ag}$. Show that the speed of A when it is vertically below O is:

$$\sqrt{V^2 + 4ag}$$

At the instant when the particle is vertically below O, it collides and coalesces with a stationary particle of mass $2m$. Assuming the string has remained taut, find the tension in the string attached to the composite particle of mass $3m$, when OA makes an angle θ with the downward vertical.

Find also the least value of V for which the composite particle describes complete vertical circles.

3 One end of a light inextensible string of length a is fixed and to the other end is attached a particle of mass m. When the particle is hanging freely at rest, it is given a horizontal velocity u so that it moves in a complete vertical circle. given that, during the motion, the minimum tension in the string is $3mg$, show that $u = \sqrt{8ag}$.

When the string is at an angle θ to the downward vertical, find, in terms of m, g and θ,

(a) the tension in the string

(b) the horizontal and vertical components of the acceleration of the particle.

4 A solid hemisphere rests with its plane face, centre O, on a horizontal table. A particle P of mass m is placed on the hemisphere at its highest point and is slightly disturbed from rest so that it begins to slide down the curved surface, the friction between the hemisphere and the particle being negligible.

If the hemisphere is fixed, show that, when the line OP has turned through an angle θ, the reaction between the hemisphere and the particle is $mg(3\cos\theta - 2)$. State the value of θ when P leaves the surface of the hemisphere.

5 Show that the velocity with which a particle hanging from a fixed point by a string of length a must be started so as to describe a complete vertical circle, must not be less than $\sqrt{5ag}$. The particle is started with a velocity of $2\sqrt{ag}$, and when the string is horizontal, is held at such a point that the particle just completes the circle. Where must the point be situated on the string?

6 A particle, of mass m, is fixed to one end A of a light inextensible string OA of length a. The other end O of the string is attached to a fixed peg. At time $t = 0$, A is vertically below O with the string taut and the particle is projected horizontally with speed V, where $V^2 > 2ag$. Show that, provided the string remains taut, the speed of the particle when it is vertically above O is $\sqrt{V^2 - 4ag}$.

Show also that the particle performs complete circular revolutions provided that $V \geq \sqrt{5ag}$.

At the instant when the particle is vertically above O, it collides and coalesces with a stationary particle, also of mass m. Find the least value of V for which the composite particle describes complete vertical circles.

Assuming the composite particle describes a complete vertical circle find, in terms of V a, m, g and θ the tension in the string when OA makes an angle θ with the downward vertical.

SUMMARY

This section has covered the principle of conservation of mechanical energy, and its application to problems involving particles moving in a vertical circle. You should now know that:

- the two main equations for systems involving vertical circular motion come from conservation of energy and the force towards the centre, $\dfrac{mv^2}{r}$ or $mr\omega^2$

- particles need a certain minimum initial velocity in order to describe complete circles and

- the minimum tension in the string occurs at the top, with the maximum at the bottom.

You should also appreciate that slightly different conditions apply when the motion is kept circular by the shape of the supporting wire or hoop.

Centre of mass

We have already seen in Module M1 how we can find the centre of masses of a number of regular shapes, including cases where shapes are added to or removed from others. We are now going to extend the range of shapes and objects for which we can find the centre of mass using the powerful tool of integration. The remainder of the section deals with an analysis of certain systems in equilibrium.

For your work on this section you will need to be familiar with:

- the material in Module M1 on centre of mass
- basic integration methods
- the idea of moments and how to take them.

Finding the centre of mass by integration

We can deduce neat formulae which give us the x- and the y-coordinates of the centre of mass in most cases using the same principle that we used in the case of composite figures, i.e.

Sum of the separate moments = Moment of the whole

We find expressions for each side of this relation and equating these

expressions gives us an equation from which we can find $\bar{x}$ or $\bar{y}$. We'll take each side in turn and see how we can find approximate expressions.

Sum of separate moments

Before we start, we have to be familiar with a way of looking at integration as the limit of a sum of small components, so that as $\delta x \to 0$,

$$\Sigma x \delta x \to \int x \, dx, \text{ for example, and } \Sigma y^2 \delta x \to \int y^2 \, dx$$

where the arrow means 'tends towards'.

We can split the method for finding our expression into 4 stages

1 Find the moment of a small strip

2 Find the sum of these moments

3 Express the limit of this sum (as the strips become narrower) as an integral

4 Evaluate the integral

Let's take as an example the thin lamina bounded by the curve $y = 4 - x^2$ and the positive x- and y-axis. To find the position of $\bar{x}$ we need to find moments about the y-axis. The diagram shows the shape together with a small strip of thickness δx taken down from the point (x, y)

Figure 7.1

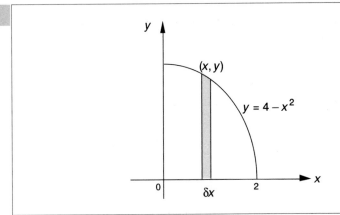

1 *Moment of strip:*

Since the height is y and the breadth δx, we can take the area to be $y\delta x$. Assuming a constant density of ρ per unit area, this gives a mass of $\rho y \delta x$. Since the strip is at a distance x from the y-axis, the moment about that axis is $\rho x y \delta x$

2 *Sum of moments:*

Dividing the whole shape into thin strips of equal thickness gives a total sum of

$$\Sigma \rho x y \delta x$$

3 *Limit of sum:*

As the strips are taken thinner, i.e. $\delta x \to 0$,

$$\sum_{\text{all}} \rho x y \delta x \quad \to \quad \int_{\text{all}} \rho x y \, dx \qquad \qquad \text{... } Ⓐ$$

4 Evaluating the integral:

The integral above is for a general curve: in the case we are looking at, $y = 4 - x^2$ and x lies between 0 and 2.

This gives the sum of the moments as

$$\int_0^2 \rho x\,(4 - x^2)\,dx \;=\; \rho \int_0^2 (4x - x^3)\,dx$$

$$= \rho \left[2x^2 - \frac{x^4}{4} \right]_0^2$$

$$= 4\rho \qquad \qquad \ldots \text{\textcircled{1}}$$

Moment of the whole

This is easier: if we assume the centre of mass is at a point $\bar{x}$ from the y-axis, the moment will be mass $\times \bar{x}$ = density $\times$ area $\times \bar{x}$

$$= \rho \bar{x} \int_{\text{all}} y\,dx \qquad \qquad \ldots \text{\textcircled{B}}$$

In our particular case, this becomes

$$\rho \bar{x} \int_0^2 (4 - x^2)\,dx \;=\; \rho \bar{x} \left[4x - \frac{x^3}{3} \right]_0^2$$

$$= \frac{16\rho\bar{x}}{3} \qquad \qquad \ldots \text{\textcircled{2}}$$

Equating ① and ② gives $\dfrac{16\rho\bar{x}}{3} = 4\rho$

$$\Rightarrow \bar{x} = \frac{3}{4}$$

Looking at the diagram of the shape, this is a reasonable result. Since there is more mass to the left, we expect $\bar{x}$ to be something less than 1.

Similarly, we would expect $\bar{y}$ to be a little less than 2. The method for calculating $\bar{y}$ is very similar: we use the same strip, only now the distance of the centre of mass of this strip from the *x-axis* will be half-way up, i.e. $\dfrac{y}{2}$.

This gives a moment for the strip about the *x*-axis as $\rho \times y\delta x \times \dfrac{y}{2} = \dfrac{\rho y^2}{2} \delta x$

and a corresponding sum of all these of

$$\Sigma \rho \frac{y^2}{2}\, \delta x$$

In the limit, as $\delta x \to 0$, this tends to $\dfrac{\rho}{2} \displaystyle\int_{\text{all}} y^2 dx \qquad \qquad \ldots \text{\textcircled{C}}$

In this case, this is $\quad \frac{1}{2}\rho \int_0^2 (4-x^2)^2\, dx$

$$= \frac{1}{2}\rho \int_0^2 (16 - 8x^2 + x^4)\, dx$$

$$= \frac{1}{2}\rho \left[16x - \frac{8x^3}{3} + \frac{x^5}{5} \right]_0^2 \qquad = \frac{128\rho}{15} \qquad \qquad \dots ③$$

The moment of the whole is as before with $\bar{y}$ instead of $\bar{x}$, i.e.

$$\rho\bar{y} \int y\, dx \qquad\qquad\qquad \dots ⑩$$

giving in this case, since $\displaystyle\int_0^2 y\, dx = \frac{16}{3}$, $\dfrac{16\rho\bar{y}}{3}$ $\qquad\qquad \dots ④$

Equating ③ and ④ gives $\dfrac{16\rho\bar{y}}{3} = \dfrac{128\rho}{15}$

$$\Rightarrow \bar{y} = \frac{8}{5}$$

which is about the prediction.

We can equate the expressions Ⓐ and Ⓑ to give a position for $\bar{x}$ for any (suitable) shape

i.e. $\quad \rho \int xy\, dx = \rho\bar{x} \int y\, dx \;\Rightarrow\; \bar{x} = \dfrac{\int xy\, dx}{\int y\, dx}$

Similarly, equating Ⓒ and Ⓓ gives $\bar{y} = \dfrac{1}{2} \dfrac{\int y^2\, dx}{\int y\, dx}$

This is an important general result …

> For (suitable) areas, the position of the centre of mass can be found from
>
> $$\bar{x} = \frac{\int xy\, dx}{\int y\, dx}, \qquad \bar{y} = \frac{\frac{1}{2}\int y^2\, dx}{\int y\, dx}$$

Volumes of revolution

Very little adjustment is needed to find the centre of mass of a volume formed by rotating a solid about the x-axis. Since the x-axis is an axis of symmetry, we only need to find $\bar{x}$. If we take a strip as before and rotate it around the x-axis, we end up with a thin disc; radius y and thickness δx.

Figure 7.2

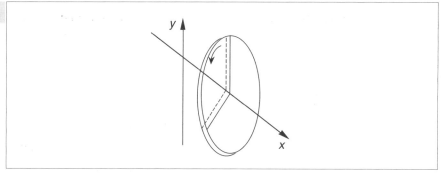

The volume of this cylinder is $\pi y^2 \delta x$, its mass is $\rho \pi y^2 \delta x$ where ρ is the density and its moment about the y-axis is $\rho \pi y^2 \delta x \times x = \rho \pi x y^2 \delta x$.

The sum of these is $\Sigma \rho \pi x y^2 \delta x$ which tends to $\rho \pi \int x y^2 dx$ as $\delta x \to 0$.

Since the volume is $\pi \int y^2 dx$, the moment of the whole about the y-axis is $\rho \pi \bar{x} \int y^2 dx$ and equating these two expressions,

$$\rho \pi \int x y^2 dx = \rho \pi \bar{x} \int y^2 dx \Rightarrow \bar{x} = \frac{\int x y^2 dx}{\int y^2 dx}$$

> For (suitable) volumes formed by rotating an area around the x-axis, the coordinates of its centre of mass are
>
> $$\bar{x} = \frac{\int x y^2 dx}{\int y^2 dx}, \qquad \bar{y} = 0$$

Standard results

The two sets of formulae, one for area and one for volume, allow us to calculate the position of the centre of mass of a number of standard figures without too much trouble.

Right-angled triangle

If we suppose a height is h and the base b we can align it with our axes as in Figure 7.3.

Figure 7.3

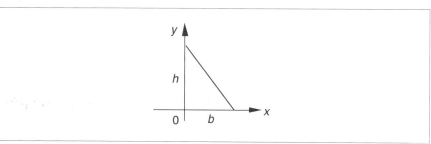

The defining line has a gradient of $-\dfrac{h}{b}$ and intercept h, and so an equation

$$y = -\frac{h}{b}x + h.$$

To find $\bar{x}$, we use $\bar{x} = \dfrac{\int xy\,dx}{\int y\,dx}$ which gives

$$\bar{x} = \frac{\displaystyle\int_0^b x\left(-\frac{h}{b}x + h\right)dx}{\displaystyle\int_0^b \left(-\frac{h}{b}x + h\right)dx} = \frac{\displaystyle\int_0^b \left(-\frac{h}{b}x^2 + hx\right)dx}{\displaystyle\int_0^b \left(-\frac{h}{b}x + h\right)dx} = \frac{\left[\dfrac{-hx^3}{3b} + \dfrac{hx^2}{2}\right]_0^b}{\left[\dfrac{-h}{2b}x^2 + hx\right]_0^b}$$

$$= \frac{\dfrac{hb^2}{3} + \dfrac{hb^2}{2}}{\dfrac{-hb}{2} + hb} = \frac{\dfrac{hb^2}{6}}{\dfrac{hb}{2}} = \frac{b}{3}$$

Similarly, we would find that $\bar{y} = \dfrac{h}{3}$

Cone

We can use the same line as in the previous case and rotate it around the x-axis. Using the formula $\bar{x} = \dfrac{\int xy^2\,dx}{\int y^2\,dx}$ gives

$$\bar{x} = \frac{\displaystyle\int_0^b x\left(-\frac{h}{b}x + h\right)^2 dx}{\displaystyle\int_0^b \left(-\frac{h}{b}x + h\right)^2 dx} = \frac{\displaystyle\int_0^b \left(\frac{h^2}{b^2}x^3 - \frac{2h^2x^2}{b} + h^2x\right)dx}{\displaystyle\int_0^b \left(\frac{h^2}{b^2}x^2 - \frac{2h^2x}{b} + h^2\right)dx}$$

$$= \frac{\left[\dfrac{h^2}{b^2}\dfrac{x^4}{4} - \dfrac{2h^2}{b}\dfrac{x^3}{3} + h^2\dfrac{x^2}{2}\right]_0^b}{\left[\dfrac{h^2}{b^2}\dfrac{x^3}{3} - \dfrac{2h^2}{b}\dfrac{x^2}{2} + h^2 x\right]_0^b} = \frac{\dfrac{h^2b^2}{4} - \dfrac{2h^2b^2}{3} + \dfrac{h^2b^2}{2}}{\dfrac{h^2b}{3} - h^2b + h^2b}$$

$$= \frac{\dfrac{h^2b^2}{12}}{\dfrac{h^2b}{3}} = \frac{b}{4}$$

i.e. the centre of mass of a cone is a quarter of the way up from the base.

Hemisphere

We can use a quadrant of a circle with radius a: if the centre of the circle is at the origin its equation will be:

$$x^2 + y^2 = a^2$$

Figure 7.4

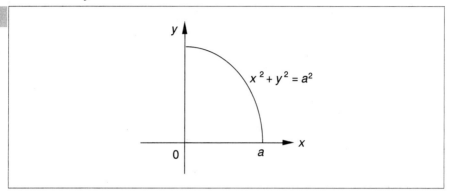

Then we have $\bar{x} = \dfrac{\int xy^2 dx}{\int y^2 dx} = \dfrac{\displaystyle\int_0^a x\,(a^2 - x^2)\ dx}{\displaystyle\int_0^a (a^2 - x^2)\ dx}$

$$= \frac{\left[a^2 \dfrac{x^2}{2} - \dfrac{x^4}{4}\right]_0^a}{\left[a^2 x - \dfrac{x^3}{3}\right]_0^a} = \frac{\dfrac{a^2}{4}}{\dfrac{2a^3}{3}} = \frac{3a}{8}$$

i.e. the centre of mass of a solid hemisphere is $\dfrac{3a}{8}$ from the centre of the sphere.

Here is a question which involves both these last results: you might like to try and remember the proofs without looking back!

Example   Prove, by integration, that

(a)   the centre of mass of a uniform solid right circular cone of height h is at a distance $\dfrac{3}{4} h$ from the vertex of the cone

(b)   the centre of mass of a uniform solid hemisphere of radius r is at a distance $\dfrac{3}{8} r$ from the centre of the plane face of the hemisphere.

Figure 7.5

A uniform solid is formed from a hemisphere of radius r and a cone of base radius r and height h, the base of the cone being coincident with the plane face of the hemisphere, as shown in the diagram. Given that the centre of mass of the solid is at a distance h from the vertex of the cone, find the numerical value of the ratio $h : r$.

Solution (a), (b) Standard results in the notes

Figure 7.6

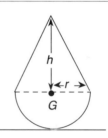

Taking moments about a diameter of the common face, on which the centre of mass (CoM) lies, of the parts gives

$$\frac{1}{3}\pi r^2 h \quad \times \quad \frac{h}{4} \quad - \quad \frac{2}{3}\pi r^3 \quad \times \quad \frac{3}{8}r \quad = \quad 0$$

Volume cone	CoM	Volume hemisphere	CoM	moment of whole

$$\Rightarrow \quad \frac{\pi r^2 h^2}{12} \quad = \quad \frac{\pi r^4}{4} \quad \Rightarrow \quad \frac{h^2}{r^2} = 3 \quad \Rightarrow \quad h : r \quad = \quad \sqrt{3} : 1$$

The next example involves the lamina being suspended by a string in the final part: if you remember from your work on M1, this means that the centre of mass is vertically below the point of suspension.

| **Example** | The diagram shows a uniform lamina of mass M, which has the shape of the region enclosed by the x-axis and the curve with equation $ay = ax - x^2$, where a is a positive constant. The centre of mass of the lamina is at G. |

Figure 7.7

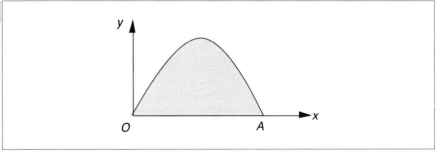

Find the coordinates of G, and prove that if the lamina were freely suspended from O, the line OA would make an angle θ with the vertical where $\tan \theta = \frac{1}{5}$.

| **Solution** | |

$$ay = ax - x^2 \Rightarrow \text{ when } y = 0, \quad ax - x^2 = 0$$
$$x(a - x) = 0$$
$$x = 0 \text{ or } x = a$$

Since a parabola is symmetrical about its turning point, the centre of mass will lie along this axis of symmetry, i.e. $\overline{x} = \dfrac{a}{2}$

Now we have $\overline{y}$

$$= \frac{\frac{1}{2}\int y^2 dx}{\int y dx} = \frac{\frac{1}{2}\int_0^a \frac{1}{a^2}\left(ax - x^2\right)^2 dx}{\int_0^a \frac{1}{a}\left(ax - x^2\right) dx}$$

$$= \frac{\dfrac{1}{2a^2}\int_0^a \left(a^2 x^2 - 2ax^3 + x^4\right) dx}{\dfrac{1}{a}\int_0^a \left(ax - x^2\right)\ dx}$$

$$= \frac{\dfrac{1}{2a^2}\left[\dfrac{a^2 x^3}{3} - \dfrac{2ax^4}{4} + \dfrac{x^5}{5}\right]_0^a}{\dfrac{1}{a}\left[\dfrac{ax^2}{2} - \dfrac{x^3}{3}\right]_0^a} = \frac{\dfrac{1}{2a^2} \times \dfrac{a^5}{30}}{\dfrac{1}{a} \times \dfrac{a^3}{6}} = \dfrac{a}{10}$$

i.e. the coordinates of G are $\left(\dfrac{a}{2}, \dfrac{a}{10}\right)$

Figure 7.8

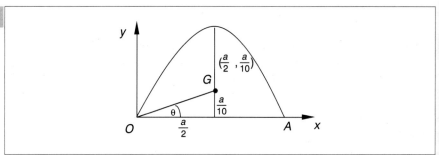

Suspended from O, OG would be vertical. Tan $\theta = \frac{a}{10} \div \frac{a}{2} = \frac{1}{5}$ as required.

You should now be able to answer Exercises 1–9 on pp. 126–129.

Object on an inclined plane

If we place an object on a plane which is initially horizontal and then start to tilt the plane at an increasing angle, eventually one of two things will happen. Either the object will start to **slip** down the plane or, if the plane and/or solid are sufficiently rough, the object will **topple**. The condition for toppling, assuming that there is no slipping, is that the vertical line through the centre of mass passes outside the point about which the object is liable to topple.

Figure 7.9

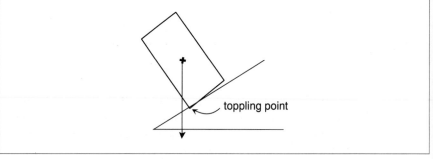

This object will topple, since the vertical lies outside the toppling point.

Figure 7.10

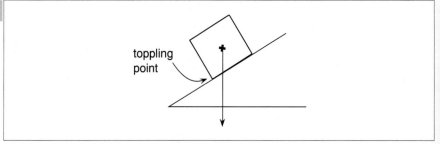

Vertical inside the toppling point, so body will not topple.

Let's try a couple of examples which use this principle.

Example

A cuboid has a square base of side 6 cm and a height of 10 cm. It is placed on an inclined plane making an angle of α to the horizontal. Find the size of α if the cuboid is on the point of toppling. (Assume the plane to be sufficiently rough to prevent slipping.)

Solution

Again, we start with a diagram.

Figure 7.11

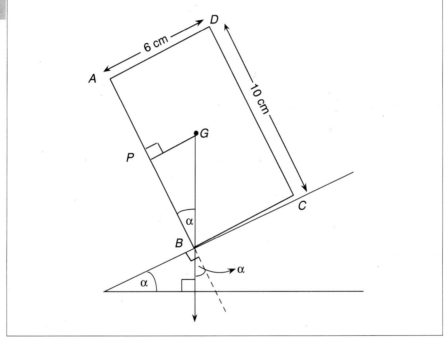

Since the cuboid is on the point of toppling, the vertical through G passes exactly through B. G is the position of the centre of mass, so that $PG = 3$ cm and $PB = 5$ cm. The angle PBG is α, the same as the angle made by the plane to the horizontal, and so

$$\tan \alpha = \frac{PG}{PB} = \frac{3}{5} \Rightarrow \alpha = 31.0° \text{ (1 d.p.)}$$

The next example starts with the proof of a standard result, the distance of the centre of mass of a triangle from its base.

Show by integration that the centre of mass of a uniform triangular lamina PQR is at a distance $\frac{1}{3}h$ from QR, where h is the length of the altitude through P.

A uniform lamina $ABCD$ is in the form of a trapezium in which $AB = AD = a$, $CD = 2a$ and $\angle BAD = \angle ADC = 90°$. Find the distance of the centre of mass of the lamina from AD and from AB.

The lamina stands with the edge AB on a plane inclined at an angle α to the horizontal with A higher than B. The lamina is in a vertical plane through a line of greatest slope of the plane. If the lamina is on the point of overturning about B, find the value of $\tan \alpha$.

We can use the standard result that we found earlier: in a right-angled triangle of height h, the centre of mass is $\frac{1}{3}h$ up from the base. Dividing the triangle into two right-angled triangles, each of height h and taking moments about the base, using

Figure 7.12

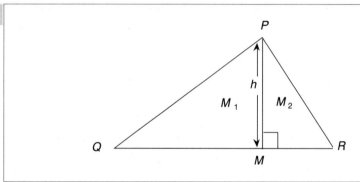

Moment whole $\quad =$ Moment $\triangle PQM +$ Moment $\triangle PMR$

$$\Rightarrow (M_1 + M_2)\,\overline{y} \quad = M_1\frac{h}{3} + M_2\frac{h}{3}$$

$$\overline{y} \quad = \frac{h}{3}\frac{(M_1 + M_2)}{M_1 + M_2} = \frac{h}{3}$$

i.e. the centre of mass for the whole triangle is at a distance of $\frac{h}{3}$ from the base QR.

We can divide the trapezium in the next part into two sections by drawing a line through B parallel to AD to meet DC at E (see Figure 7.13).

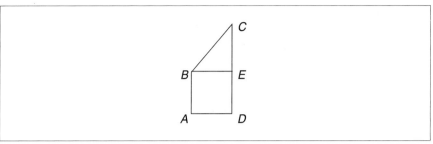

Figure 7.13

Then from what we have just shown, the centre of mass of the triangle BEC will be one third of the way up EC from BE, i.e. $\frac{a}{3}$ from BE or $\frac{4a}{3}$ from AD.

Similarly it will be one third of the way up EB from CE, i.e. $\frac{a}{3}$ from CE or $\frac{2a}{3}$ from AB.

We'll set up tables for moments about AB and about AD, with ρ being the mass per unit area.

Moments about AB

	Area	Mass	CoM	Moment
$ABDE$	a^2	$a^2\rho$	$\frac{a}{2}$	$\frac{a^3\rho}{2}$
BEC	$\frac{a^2}{2}$	$\frac{a^2\rho}{2}$	$\frac{2a}{3}$	$\frac{a^3\rho}{3}$
Whole	$\frac{3a^2}{2}$	$\frac{3a^2\rho}{2}$	$\bar{x}$	$\frac{3a^2\rho\bar{x}}{2}$

Equating moments, $\quad \dfrac{3a^2\rho\bar{x}}{2} = \dfrac{a^3\rho}{3} + \dfrac{a^3\rho}{2} = \dfrac{5a^3\rho}{6}$

$$\Rightarrow \bar{x} = \frac{5a}{9} \qquad\qquad \dots ④$$

Moments about AD

	Area	Mass	CoM	Moment
$ABDE$	a^2	$a^2\rho$	$\frac{a}{2}$	$\frac{a^3\rho}{2}$
BEC	$\frac{a^2}{2}$	$\frac{a^2\rho}{2}$	$\frac{4a}{3}$	$\frac{2a^3\rho}{3}$
Whole	$\frac{3a^2}{2}$	$\frac{3a^2\rho}{2}$	$\bar{y}$	$\frac{3a^2\rho\bar{y}}{2}$

Then $\quad \dfrac{3a^2\rho\bar{y}}{2} = \dfrac{a^3\rho}{2} + 2\dfrac{a^3\rho}{3} = \dfrac{7a^3\rho}{6} \quad \Rightarrow \bar{y} = \dfrac{7a}{9} \qquad \dots ⑤$

Figure 7.14

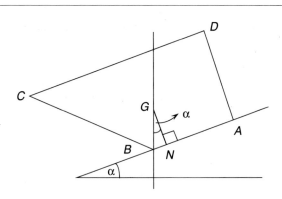

Since the lamina is on the point of overturning, the centre of mass, at G say must be vertically above B. If we draw in the normal from G,

then $\quad GN = \dfrac{5a}{9}$ (using ④)

and $\quad BN = a - \dfrac{7a}{9} = \dfrac{2a}{9}$ (using ⑤).

Then $\quad \tan \alpha = \dfrac{BN}{GN} = \dfrac{\frac{2a}{9}}{\frac{5a}{9}} = \dfrac{2}{5}$

Objects suspended by two strings

To find the tension in each of the strings, we take moments about the axis through one string and then the axis through the other.

Figure 7.15

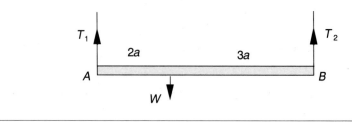

The diagram shows a non-uniform plank AB of length $5a$ with its centre of mass $2a$ from one end.

Moments about the vertical through A : $2aW = 5aT_2 \implies T_2 = \dfrac{2}{5}W$ ... ⑥

Moments about the vertical through B : $3aW = 5aT_1 \implies T_1 = \dfrac{3}{5}W$ ... ⑦

Note that the forces on the plank are in equilibrium, i.e. $T_1 + T_2 = W$, which we could have used instead of ② to find T_1. Here's an example of this idea.

Example

From a uniform solid right circular cone of height H is removed a cone with the same base and of height h, the two axes coinciding. Show that the centre of mass of the remaining solid S is a distance

$$\frac{1}{4}(3H - h)$$

from the vertex of the original cone.

The solid S is suspended by two vertical strings, one attached to the vertex and the other attached to a point on the bounding circular base. Given that S is in equilibrium, with its axis of symmetry horizontal, find, in terms of H and h, the ratio of the magnitude of the tension in the string attached to the vertex to that in the other string.

Solution

See Figure 7.16.

Figure 7.16

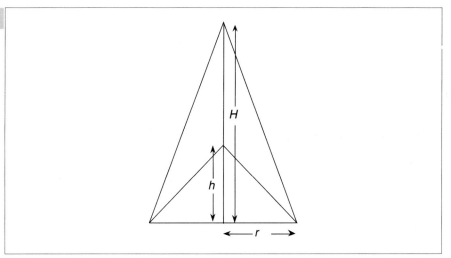

The centre of mass of a right circular cone is a quarter of the height above the base

Large cone :   Vol is $\frac{1}{3}\pi r^2 H$ $\Rightarrow$ moment is $\frac{1}{3}\pi r^2 H\rho \times \dfrac{H}{4}$

Small cone :   Vol is $\frac{1}{3}\pi r^2 h$ $\Rightarrow$ moment is $\frac{1}{3}\pi r^2 h\rho \times \dfrac{h}{4}$

Remainder :   Vol is $\frac{1}{3}\pi r^2(H - h)$ $\Rightarrow$ moment is $\frac{1}{3}\pi r^2(H - h)\rho \times \bar{y}$

Moment of large = moment of small + moment of remainder

$$\frac{1}{3}\pi r^2 H\rho \times \frac{H}{4} = \frac{1}{3}\pi r^2 h\rho \times \frac{h}{4} + \frac{1}{3}\pi r^2(H - h)\rho\bar{y}$$

$$\Rightarrow (H-h)\bar{y} = \frac{H^2}{4} - \frac{h^2}{4} = \frac{1}{4}(H^2 - h^2)$$

$$\Rightarrow \bar{y} = \frac{1}{4}\frac{H^2 - h^2}{H - h} = \frac{1}{4}(H + h)$$

So from the vertex of the original cone, the centre of mass will be

$$H - \bar{y} = H - \frac{1}{4}(H + h) = H - \frac{1}{4}H - \frac{1}{4}h = \frac{3}{4}H - \frac{1}{4}h$$

$$= \frac{1}{4}(3H - h)$$

Figure 7.17

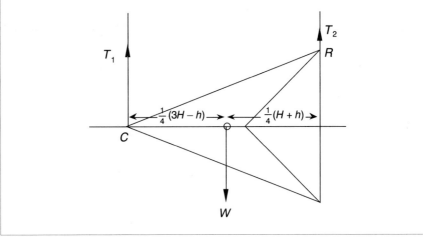

Taking moments about the **vertical axis** through C,

$$W \times \frac{1}{4}(3H - h) = T_2 H \qquad \qquad \dots \text{①}$$

Moments about **vertical axis** through R,

$$W \times \frac{1}{4}(H + h) = T_1 H \qquad \qquad \dots \text{②}$$

Dividing ② by ① $\dfrac{T_1 H}{T_2 H} = \dfrac{W \times \frac{1}{4}(H + h)}{W \times \frac{1}{4}(3H - h)} \Rightarrow \dfrac{T_1}{T_2} = \dfrac{H + h}{3H - h}$

Systems in equilibrium

To conclude the section, we are going to have a look at the way in which we can apply our knowledge of the position of the centre of mass to work out details of some simple systems in equilibrium.

A very popular question of this type involves a ladder leaning up against a wall. Here is a typical example.

Example

A ladder, *AB*, of length 2*l* and weight *W*, is in equilibrium with the end *A* on a rough horizontal floor and the end *B* against a smooth vertical wall. The ladder makes an angle $\tan^{-1} 2$ with the horizontal and is in a vertical plane which is perpendicular to the wall. By modelling the ladder as a uniform rod, find the least possible value of μ, the coefficient of friction between the floor and the ladder.

Given that $\mu = \frac{5}{16}$, find the distance from *A* of the highest point of the ladder to which a man of weight *W* can climb without disturbing equilibrium. Model the man as a particle.

Solution

The first step is to mark in the forces acting on the ladder.

Figure 7.18

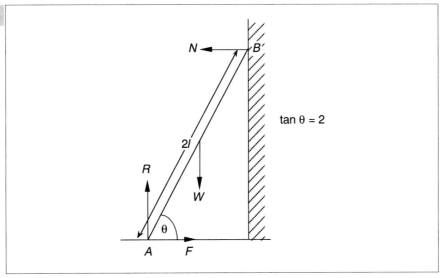

The force at *B* is just a normal reaction since the wall is smooth, whereas at *A* there is a normal reaction and a frictional force, since the ground is rough. Note that we don't put μR for the friction: this is the *maximum* possible friction and only applies in *limiting* equilibrium. The next step is to see where our equations will come from. There are 4 choices: resolving vertically and horizontally and taking moments about *A* or *B*.

In this case, since we're not interested in the normal reaction at *B* we can take moments about *B* and also resolve vertically.

Moments about *B*: $R \times 2l \cos \theta - Wl \cos \theta - F \times 2l \sin \theta = 0$

$\Rightarrow 2lF \sin \theta = 2lR \cos \theta - WlR \cos \theta$

$\div$ by $l \cos \theta$ $2F \tan \theta = 2R - W$

$\tan \theta = 2$ $4F = 2R - W$ ... ①

Vertical forces: $\qquad R = W$ ... ②

① into ② gives $\qquad 4F = 2W - W = W$

$$\Rightarrow F = \frac{W}{4}$$

since $F \leq \mu R,\ \mu R \geq \dfrac{W}{4} \ \Rightarrow\ \mu W \geq \dfrac{W}{4} \ \Rightarrow\ \mu \geq \dfrac{1}{4}$

Figure 7.19

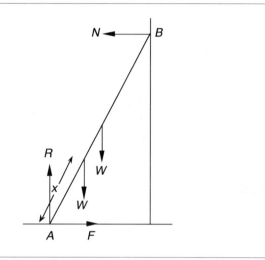

x is the distance that the man is from A

The same equations will serve for the second part:

About B: $\qquad 2lR \cos\theta - Wl \cos\theta - W(2l - x)\cos\theta - 2lF \sin\theta = 0$

$\div$ by $l \cos\theta \qquad 2R - W - 2W + \dfrac{Wx}{l} - 2F \tan\theta = 0 \qquad$ ... ③

Vertically: $\qquad R = 2W$ ...④

and then ③ becomes

$$4W - W - 2W + \frac{Wx}{l} = 2F \tan\theta = 4F \ \Rightarrow\ 4F = W + \frac{Wx}{l} \qquad \text{... ⑤}$$

But $F \leq \mu R = 2\mu W = 2 \times \dfrac{5}{16} W = \dfrac{5W}{8} \ \Rightarrow\ 4F \leq \dfrac{5W}{2}$

$\qquad$ ⑤ $\qquad$ becomes $4F = W + \dfrac{Wx}{l} \leq \dfrac{5W}{2}$

$$\Rightarrow \frac{Wx}{l} \leq \frac{3W}{2}$$

$$\Rightarrow x \leq \frac{3l}{2}$$

i.e. the highest point he can climb is $\dfrac{3l}{2}$ from A.

Here is another example, similar except for the fact that the rod is supported by an elastic string instead of a wall: this time we are interested in the upper forces rather than the lower forces and we take moments about the bottom.

Example

A uniform rod AB, of length $2a$ and mass m, rests in equilibrium with its lower end A on a rough horizontal floor. Equilibrium is maintained by a horizontal elastic string, of natural length a and modulus λ. One end of the string is attached to B and the other end to a point vertically above A.

Given that θ, where $\theta < \frac{\pi}{3}$, is the inclination of the rod to the horizontal, show that the magnitude of the tension in the string is $\frac{1}{2} mg \cot \theta$.

Prove also that:

$$2\lambda = \frac{(mg \cot \theta)}{(2 \cos \theta - 1)}$$

Solution

Figure 7.20

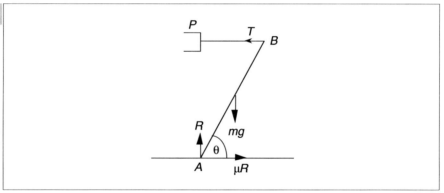

The quickest way of finding T is by taking moments about R: this involves finding the components of the forces perpendicular to the rod.

Figure 7.21

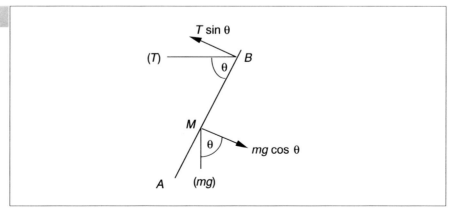

You have to be careful to sort out which of the angles is θ: having done this, the forces are $mg \cos θ$ at M, i.e. a from A and $T \sin θ$ in the opposite direction at B, i.e. $2a$ from A Then taking moments

$$mg \cos θ \, (a) - T \sin θ \, (2a) = 0$$
$$\Rightarrow T \sin θ \, (2a) = mg \cos θ \, (a)$$
$$\Rightarrow T = \frac{mg \cos θ}{2 \sin θ} = \frac{1}{2} mg \cot θ$$

For the next part, we need to find the length of the elastic string so that we can determine the extension and hence the tension.

Figure 7.22

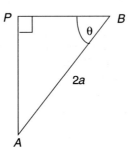

The length of the string, PB, is $2a \cos θ \Rightarrow$ since the natural length is a, the extension is $2a \cos θ - a = a \, (2 \cos θ - 1)$. This gives the tension as

$$T = \frac{λx}{a} = \frac{λa \, (2 \cos θ - 1)}{a} = λ \, (2 \cos θ - 1)$$

But since we know that $T = \frac{1}{2} mg \cot θ$,

$$λ \, (2 \cos θ - 1) = \frac{1}{2} mg \cot θ$$
$$\Rightarrow 2λ = \frac{mg \cot θ}{2 \cos θ - 1}$$

You should now be able to answer Exercises 10–11 on pp. 129–130.

EXERCISES

1 A uniform lamina has the shape of the region enclosed by the x-axis and the part of the curve $y = x \, (2 - x)$ for which $0 \le x \le 2$. Find the coordinates of the centre of mass of the lamina.

2 The diagram shows part of the curve $y = x^2 + 1$ between $x = 0$ and $x = 1$. Find the coordinates of the centre of mass of the solid obtained when this area is rotated 360° around the x-axis.

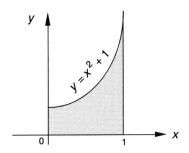

3 The diagram shows a vertical section through the centres of three uniform cubical blocks which are glued together. The cubes all have the same density. The lowest cube, cross-section $ABCD$, has edge $3a$, the middle one has edge $2a$ and the uppermost one has edge a. Referred to AB and AD, as axes of x and y respectively, the centre of mass has coordinates $(\bar{x}, \bar{y})$.

Show that $\bar{x} = \frac{29}{18}a$ and find $\bar{y}$ in terms of a.

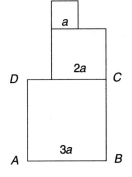

The composite solid is placed, with AB along a line of greatest slope and with B above A, on a rough plane inclined at an angle a to the horizontal. Find $\tan \alpha$, given that the solid is on the point of toppling.

(Note that they are *cubes* and not just squares!)

4 Show that the centre of mass of a uniform hemisphere is at a distance $\frac{3}{8}r$ from the centre of the plane face, where r is the radius.

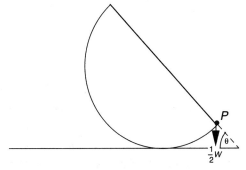

A uniform solid hemisphere of weight W is placed with its spherical surface on a smooth horizontal plane. A particle P of weight $\frac{1}{2}W$ is attached to its rim. In the position of equilibrium the plane face of the hemisphere is inclined at an angle θ to the horizontal, as shown in the diagram. Find $\tan \theta$.

5

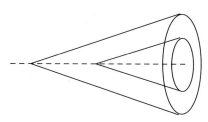

Show that the centre of mass of a uniform solid right circular cone of height h and base-radius a is at a distance $\frac{3}{4}h$ from the vertex.

A hole in the shape of a right circular cone of base-radius $\frac{1}{2}a$ and height $\frac{2}{3}h$ is bored out of this cone; the axis of the hole coincides with that of the cone. The resulting solid is shown in the diagram. Find the distance of the centre of mass of this solid from the vertex of the original cone.

6 A uniform circular cylinder has height h and radius r. From the cylinder, a cone C, with vertex O at the centre of one plane end of the cylinder and with the other plane end as base, is removed. Show that the distance of the centre of mass of the remaining solid R from O is $\frac{3}{8}h$.
(The position of the centre of mass of a cone may be quoted without proof.)

The plane circular faces of C and R are now glued together, with their circumferences coincident, and the resulting body is suspended in equilibrium from a point on the circumference of their common plane face. Given that $h = 2r$, find the tangent of the angle between the axis of symmetry of the body and the horizontal.

7 (a) Prove, by integration, that the centre of mass of a uniform solid right circular cone of height h is at a distance $\frac{3}{4}h$ from the vertex V of the cone.

(b) From this cone, which has base radius $4r$, a smaller cone, of height $\frac{1}{4}h$ and vertex V, is removed by cutting along a plane parallel to the base of the cone. Find the height above the base of the centre of mass of the frustum remaining.

(c) This frustum, which has weight W, is placed with its smaller plane face in contact with a rough horizontal table. A horizontal force of magnitude P is applied to a point on the curved surface of the frustum, the line of action of P passing through the centre of mass of the frustum. The value of P is gradually increased from zero. Given that $h = 6r$ and that the table is sufficiently rough for equilibrium to be broken by the overturning of the frustum, find, in terms of W, the value of P for which this occurs.

8 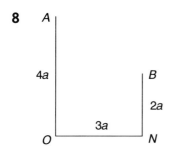 A uniform straight wire *AB*, of length 9*a*, is bent through 90° at the point *O*, where *OA* = 4*a*, and also at *N*, where *NB* = 2*a*, as shown in the diagram. The four points *A*, *O*, *N* and *B* are coplanar. Show that the distance, $\bar{x}$, of the centre of mass of the bent wire from *OA* is given by $\bar{x} = \dfrac{7}{6} a$ and find $\bar{y}$, the distance of the centre of mass from *ON*.

The bent wire is freely suspended from *B* and hangs in equilibrium. Find the tangent of the angle of inclination of *BN* to the vertical.

9 Show by integration that the centre of mass of a uniform solid right circular cone of height *h* is at a distance $\dfrac{3}{4} h$ from the vertex.

Two uniform solid right circular cones, each with the same base radius *a* and the same density, have heights *h* and *λh*, where *λ* > 1. These cones are joined together, with their circular bases coinciding, to form a spindle. Show that the centre of mass of this spindle is at a distance $\dfrac{1}{4} h (3λ + 1)$ from the vertex of the larger cone.

Given that *a* = *h*, show that the spindle can rest in equilibrium with the curved surface of the smaller cone in contact with a horizontal plane provided that *λ* ≤ 5.

10 A uniform rod *AB* of weight *W* and length 4*a* rests in a vertical plane with its end *A* on a rough horizontal plane and a point *C* of the rod, where *AC* = 3*a*, in contact with a smooth peg. If the rod makes an angle *θ* with the horizontal, show that the force exerted by the peg on the rod is $\dfrac{2}{3} W \cos θ$ and find, in terms of *W* and *θ*, the normal and frictional components of the force exerted by the plane on the rod at *A*. Deduce that, for equilibrium to be possible, the coefficient of friction *μ* between the rod and the plane at *A* cannot be less than

$$\frac{\sin 2θ}{2 - \cos 2θ}.$$

11

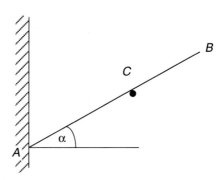

The diagram shows a uniform rod AB, of length $2l$ and mass M, which rests at an angle α to the horizontal with the end A against a rough vertical wall and with a point C in AB, where $AC = \lambda l$, resting on a smooth horizontal rail. The rod is in a vertical plane perpendicular to the wall and the rail is parallel to the wall. Given that the frictional force acting on the rod at the wall acts upwards, show that $\lambda > \cos^2 \alpha$.

SUMMARY

This section has dealt with the use of integration in finding the centre of mass of plane laminas and solids, as well as using the knowledge of the position of the centre of mass to solve problems involving systems in equilibrium. You should now:

- be able to derive the position of the centre of mass of standard laminas and solids
- know that the centre of mass lies along any axis of symmetry of a lamina or solid
- be able to take moments about a suitable axis to solve problems involving additional forces acting on a figure
- know the condition for toppling to occur
- be able to resolve forces in a suitable direction and/or take moments to solve systems in equilibrium.

MODULE

M2

Solutions

Section 1

1 (a) The bottom of the fraction can be factorised:

$$v^2 + 3v + 2 = (v + 2)(v + 1)$$

The integral becomes

$$\int \frac{v\,dv}{(v + 2)(v + 1)} = \int \left(\frac{2}{v + 2} - \frac{1}{v + 1}\right) dv$$

$$= 2\ln|v + 2| - \ln|v + 1| + C$$

$$= \ln \frac{(v + 2)^2}{|v + 1|} + C$$

(b) By division,

$$
\begin{array}{r}
1 \\
v - 2 \overline{) \; v } \\
\underline{v - 2} \\
2
\end{array}
$$

$$\frac{v}{v - 2} = 1 + \frac{2}{v - 2}$$

and the integral becomes

$$\int \frac{v}{v - 2}\,dv = \int \left(1 + \frac{2}{v - 2}\right) dv$$

$$= v + 2\ln|v - 2| + C$$

(c) Since $1 - 3v^2$ differentiates to $-6v$,

$\ln(1 - 3v^2)$ differentiates to $\dfrac{-6v}{1 - 3v^2}$

$$\Rightarrow \int \frac{-6v\,dv}{1 - 3v^2} = \ln|1 - 3v^2|$$

$$\Rightarrow \int \frac{v\,dv}{1 - 3v^2} = -\tfrac{1}{6}\ln|1 - 3v^2| + C$$

2 We want an expression connecting v and t, so we choose a to be $\dfrac{dv}{dt}$.

Then $\dfrac{dv}{dt} = 6e^{-3t}$

$$\Rightarrow \int dv = \int 6e^{-3t}\,dt$$

$$v = -2e^{-3t} + C$$

When $t = 0$, $v = 1$, and so $1 = -2 + C$

$$\Rightarrow C = 3$$

and $v = 3 - 2e^{-3t}$

When $v = 2$, $2 = 3 - 2e^{-3t} \Rightarrow 2e^{-3t} = 1$

$$\Rightarrow e^{-3t} = 0.5$$

Taking ln's of both sides, $-3t = \ln 0.5$

$$\Rightarrow t = \tfrac{1}{3}\ln 2 \text{ or } 0.23 \text{ (2 d.p.)}$$

Since $v = 3 - 2e^{-3t}$, and $2e^{-3t}$ becomes very small as t becomes large, v tends to a limiting value of 3 m s^{-1}

3 Since the first part of the question involves **displacement** and not time, we use the form $v\dfrac{dv}{dx}$ for the acceleration and write

$$v\frac{dv}{dx} = \frac{k}{v}$$

where x is the displacement from O. Rearranging this as a separable variables differential equation,

$$\int v^2\,dv = \int k\,dx$$

i.e. $\dfrac{v^3}{3} = kx + C$ \qquad ... ①

When the particle is at O, i.e. when $x = 0$, we're told that $v = 1$ m s^{-1} and so

$$\frac{1}{3} = C$$

and ① can be rewritten

$$\frac{v^3}{3} = kx + \frac{1}{3}$$ \qquad ... ②

Now we have that when $x = 13$, $v = 3$

$$\therefore \quad \frac{27}{3} = 13k + \frac{1}{3} \Rightarrow 13k = \frac{26}{3} \Rightarrow k = \frac{2}{3}$$

and ② becomes

$$\frac{v^3}{3} = \frac{2x}{3} + \frac{1}{3}$$

or $\quad v^3 = 2x + 1$ \qquad ... ③

131

When $x = 62$, $v^3 = 124 + 1 = 125$

$$\Rightarrow v = 5 \text{ m s}^{-1}$$

For the next part of the question we use the alternative form for the acceleration, $\dfrac{dv}{dt}$ and write

$$\frac{dv}{dt} = \frac{k}{v} = \frac{2}{3v} \text{ from previous part}$$

$$\Rightarrow \int v\, dv = \frac{2}{3}\int dt$$

$$\frac{v^2}{2} = \frac{2t}{3} + C$$

Initially, i.e. $t = 0$, the velocity is 1 m s^{-1}, so that

$$C = \frac{1}{2} \quad \text{and} \quad \frac{v^2}{2} = \frac{2t}{3} + \frac{1}{2}$$

Since at A we've found that $v = 5$, the time t taken to reach this point is given by

$$\frac{25}{2} = \frac{2t}{3} + \frac{1}{2}$$

$$\frac{2t}{3} = \frac{25}{2} - \frac{1}{2} = 12$$

i.e. $t = 18$ secs

4 We have first to find the speed,

using $a = \dfrac{dv}{dt}$

$$a = 3e^{2t} \Rightarrow \frac{dv}{dt} = 3e^{2t} \Rightarrow v = \frac{3}{2}e^{2t} + C$$

Given that $v = 8$ when $t = 0 \Rightarrow 8 = \dfrac{3}{2} + C$

$$\Rightarrow C = \frac{13}{2}$$

$$v = \frac{3}{2}e^{2t} + \frac{13}{2}$$

Now we need distance, using $v = \dfrac{ds}{dt}$

$$\frac{ds}{dt} = \frac{3}{2}e^{2t} + \frac{13}{2}$$

$$\Rightarrow s = \frac{3}{4}e^{2t} + \frac{13t}{2} + D$$

$s = 0$ when $t = 0 \Rightarrow$

$$0 = \frac{3}{4} + D \Rightarrow D = -\frac{3}{4}$$

$$s = \frac{3}{4}e^{2t} + \frac{13t}{2} - \frac{3}{4}$$

When $t = 2$,

$$s = \frac{3}{4}e^4 + 13 - \frac{3}{4} = 53.2 \text{ m (3 s.f.)}$$

5 Resisting force i.e. $F = -ma = -km(2u - v)$

Using $a = v\dfrac{dv}{dx}$, $\qquad a = v\dfrac{dv}{dx} = -k(2u - v)$

$$\int \frac{v\, dv}{2u - v} = \int -k\, dx$$

Dividing the fraction on the left-hand side:

$$
\begin{array}{r}
-1 \\
-v + 2u \enclose{longdiv}{ v } \\
v - 2u \\
\hline
+ 2u
\end{array}
$$

gives $\dfrac{v}{2u - v} = -1 + \dfrac{2u}{2u - v}$

i.e. $\displaystyle\int\left(-1 + \frac{2u}{2u - v}\right) dv = \int -k\, dx$

$-v - 2u \ln(2u - v) = -kx + C$

$x = 0, v = u \Rightarrow$

$-u - 2u \ln u = C$

$\Rightarrow -v - 2u \ln(2u - v) = -kx - u - 2u \ln u$

When $v = 0$, $-2u \ln 2u = -kx - u - 2u \ln u$

$kx = 2u \ln 2u - 2u \ln u - kx$

$\quad = 2u \ln 2 - u$

$\quad = u(2 \ln 2 - 1)$

$\quad = u(\ln 4 - 1) \qquad$ since $2 \ln 2 = \ln 2^2$

i.e. $x = \dfrac{u}{k}(\ln 4 - 1)$

6 We are given a **force** and it **opposes** the motion, so that it is negative. Our preliminary equation is

$$F = ma$$

$$\Rightarrow -k\sqrt{v} = ma \qquad\qquad\qquad \ldots\text{①}$$

In fact there are two parts to the question, but the first part asks for v in terms of t so we use

$$a = \frac{dv}{dt}$$

① becomes $m\dfrac{dv}{dt} = -k\sqrt{v} \qquad\qquad \ldots\text{②}$

and rearranging, $\displaystyle\int \frac{dv}{\sqrt{v}} = \int -\frac{k}{m} dt$

or $\displaystyle\int v^{-1/2}\, dv = -\frac{k}{m}\int dt$

$$\Rightarrow 2v^{1/2} = -\frac{kt}{m} + C \qquad\qquad \ldots\text{③}$$

When $t = 0$, $v = U$ and we have

$$2\sqrt{U} = C$$

and putting this back into ③ gives

$$2\sqrt{v} = \frac{-kt}{m} + 2\sqrt{U} \qquad \ldots ④$$

$$\sqrt{v} = \sqrt{U} - \frac{kt}{2m}$$

so $\quad v = \left(\sqrt{U} - \frac{kt}{2m}\right)^2$

The question continues by asking the **distance** when the particle comes to rest so we have to use $v\frac{dv}{dx}$ in place of $\frac{dv}{dt}$, and equation ② becomes

$$mv\frac{dv}{dx} = -k\sqrt{v} \qquad \ldots ②$$

$$\int \frac{v\,dv}{\sqrt{v}} = \int \frac{-k}{m}\,dx$$

$$\int v^{1/2}\,dv = \frac{-k}{m}\int dx$$

$$\frac{2}{3}v^{3/2} = \frac{-kx}{m} + C \qquad \ldots ③$$

When $\quad x = 0, v = U \Rightarrow C = \frac{2}{3}U^{3/2}$

$$\frac{2}{3}v^{3/2} = \frac{-kx}{m} + \frac{2}{3}U^{3/2} \qquad \ldots ④$$

Finally, at rest $v = 0$ and so

$$0 = \frac{-kx}{m} + \frac{2}{3}U^{3/2}$$

i.e. $\quad x = \dfrac{2mU^{3/2}}{3k}$ as required

7

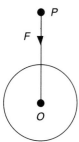

There's a temptation when thinking about forces acting on the particle in a case like this to assume that gravity is acting in the normal way, i.e. that there is an additional force of mg acting 'downwards'. In fact, there is only the given force acting – this would reduce to mg in the particular case that $x = R$, i.e. the particle is on the surface of the earth.

Since this is given as a **force** and not an acceleration, we use $F = ma$ and as we are taking the direction $\overrightarrow{OP}$, i.e. **away** from the centre of the earth, to be positive, this force, which is **towards** the centre of the earth, will be negative. We can now put down our preliminary equation

$$F = ma = -\frac{mg\,R^2}{x^2} \qquad \ldots ①$$

Looking at the question, we see it asks for the distance travelled, so for a we use the form $v\frac{dv}{dx}$ and our equation becomes

$$mv\frac{dv}{dx} = \frac{-mg\,R^2}{x^2} \qquad \ldots ②$$

Dividing through by m and rearranging our differential equation

$$\int v\,dv = \int \frac{-gR^2}{x^2}\,dx$$

$$= gR^2 \int \left(-\frac{1}{x^2}\right)dx$$

since g, R are constants

$$= gR^2 \int (-x^{-2})\,dx$$

$$\Rightarrow \frac{v^2}{2} = gR^2(x^{-1}) + C$$

$$= \frac{gR^2}{x} + C \qquad \ldots ③$$

We have to be a bit careful here – since it is projected from the surface of the earth and the distance is measured from O, the centre of the earth, the initial distance $x = R$ when $v = \sqrt{gR}$.

Putting these into ③ gives

$$\frac{gR}{2} = \frac{gR^2}{R} + C \Rightarrow C = -\frac{gR}{2}$$

giving our particular solution as

$$\frac{v^2}{2} = \frac{gR^2}{x} - \frac{gR}{2} \qquad \ldots ④$$

We want to find x when $v = \frac{1}{2}\sqrt{gR}$.

Substituting this value for v gives

$$\frac{1}{2}\left(\frac{gR}{4}\right) = \frac{gR^2}{x} - \frac{gR}{2}$$

$$\Rightarrow \frac{gR^2}{x} = \frac{gR}{2} + \frac{gR}{8} = \frac{5gR}{8}$$

$$\Rightarrow x = \frac{8R}{5}$$

The final hurdle is to note that the question asks for the **distance travelled** and not distance from the centre. Since x was R initially, the distance travelled is

$$\frac{8R}{5} - R = \frac{3R}{5}$$

8 Since the distance is measured in the positive x-direction from O, we have to take this as our positive direction for the velocity and the acceleration. The initial direction of the velocity is **towards** O, so this will be negative; the acceleration is initially **away** from O and so this will be positive.

$$a = \frac{k}{2x^2} + \frac{k}{4a^2} \qquad \dots \text{①}$$

We want to connect v and x, so we use

$$a = v\frac{dv}{dx}$$

$$v\frac{dv}{dx} = \frac{k}{2x^2} + \frac{k}{4a^2}$$

$$\int v\,dv = \int \left(\frac{k}{2x^2} + \frac{k}{4a^2}\right)dx$$

$$\frac{v^2}{2} = -\frac{k}{2x} + \frac{kx}{4a^2} + C \qquad \dots \text{②}$$

The particle passes through A, $x = 2a$, with a speed of $\sqrt{\dfrac{k}{a}}$ towards O, i.e. $v = -\sqrt{\dfrac{k}{a}}$. Putting these into ②

$$\frac{k}{2a} = -\frac{k}{4a} + \frac{k \times 2a}{4a^2} + C$$

$$\Rightarrow \ C = \frac{k}{4a} \text{ and this back in ② gives}$$

$$\frac{v^2}{2} = -\frac{k}{2x} + \frac{kx}{4a^2} + \frac{k}{4a}$$

Now when the particle is at B, where $x = a$,

$$\frac{v^2}{2} = -\frac{k}{2a} + \frac{ka}{4a^2} + \frac{k}{4a} = 0$$

Now the acceleration changes and our new equation is

$$v\frac{dv}{dx} = \frac{k}{2x^2} - \frac{k}{4a^2}$$

$$\int v\,dv = \int \left(\frac{k}{2x^2} - \frac{k}{4a^2}\right)dx$$

$$\frac{v^2}{2} = -\frac{k}{2x} - \frac{kx}{4a^2} + C \qquad \dots \text{③}$$

But at B, where $x = a$, the particle was at rest, $v = 0$

$$0 = \frac{-k}{2a} - \frac{ka}{4a^2} + C \ \Rightarrow \ C = \frac{3k}{4a}$$

and ③ becomes

$$\frac{v^2}{2} = \frac{-k}{2x} - \frac{kx}{4a^2} + \frac{3k}{4a} \qquad \dots \text{④}$$

$$= -\frac{k}{4a^2x}\left[2a^2 + x^2 - 3ax\right]$$

$$= \frac{-k}{4a^2x}\left[(x-a)(x-2a)\right]$$

So when $v = 0$, either

$$x - a = 0 \text{ or } x - 2a = 0$$

$$x = a \text{ (which is where it starts at } B)$$

or $x = 2a$, i.e. at A, the next point where it comes instantaneously to rest.

9 (a) $v\dfrac{dv}{dx} = 6x - 4x^3 \ dx$

$$\Rightarrow \ \int v\,dv = \int (6x - 4x^3)\ dx$$

$$\frac{v^2}{2} = 3x^2 - x^4 + C$$

$$x = 1, v = 0$$

$$\Rightarrow \ 0 = 3 - 1 + C \ \Rightarrow \ C = -2$$

$$\frac{v^2}{2} = 3x^2 - x^4 - 2$$

When $x = \sqrt{2}$,

$$\frac{v^2}{2} = 3 \times 2 - 4 - 2 = 0 \ \Rightarrow \ v = 0$$

(b) $\dfrac{dv}{dt} = -v^4 \ \Rightarrow \ \int \dfrac{-1}{v^4}\,dv = \int dt$

$$\frac{1}{3v^3} = t + C$$

$$v = 2 \text{ when } t = 0$$

$$\Rightarrow \ \frac{1}{24} = C \ \Rightarrow \ t = \frac{1}{3v^3} - \frac{1}{24}$$

$$v\frac{dv}{dx} = -v^4 \ \Rightarrow \ \int \frac{-1}{v^3}\,dv = \int dx$$

$$\frac{1}{2v^2} = x + C$$

$$v = 2 \text{ when } x = 0$$

$$\Rightarrow \ \frac{1}{8} = C \ \Rightarrow x = \frac{1}{2v^2} - \frac{1}{8}$$

When $v = 1$, $t = \dfrac{1}{3} - \dfrac{1}{24} = \dfrac{7}{24}$

and $x = \dfrac{1}{2} - \dfrac{1}{8} = \dfrac{3}{8}$

$$\Rightarrow \ \text{Average speed is } \frac{\frac{3}{8}}{\frac{7}{24}} = \frac{3}{8} \times \frac{24}{7} = \frac{9}{7}$$

10 (a) $\dfrac{dv}{dt} = -0.2v \Rightarrow \displaystyle\int \dfrac{dv}{v} = \int -0.2dt$

$\ln v = -0.2t + C \qquad t = 0,\ v = 24$

$\Rightarrow \ln 24 = C$

$\Rightarrow \ln v = -0.2t + \ln 24$

$\Rightarrow \ln v - \ln 24 = -0.2t$

$\ln \dfrac{v}{24} = -0.2t$

$\dfrac{v}{24} = e^{-0.2t}$

$v = 24e^{-0.2t}$

(b) $F = ma = m(-0.2v) = 0.5(-0.2 \times 24e^{-0.2t})$

$\qquad = -2.4e^{-0.2t}$

(c) $v\dfrac{dv}{ds} = -0.2v$

$\Rightarrow v = -0.2s + C;\qquad s = 0,\ v = 24$

$24 = C$

$\Rightarrow v = 24 - 0.2s$

(d) (i) When $v = 12,\ 12 = 24 - 0.2s$

$0.2s = 24 - 12 = 12$

$s = 60$ m

(ii) $v = 12,\quad 12 = 24e^{-0.2t}$

$0.5 = e^{-0.2t}$

$\ln 0.5 = -0.2t$

$t = -5 \ln 0.5 = 5 \ln 2$

$\left(\text{since } -\ln \dfrac{1}{2} = \ln 2\right)$

11 (a) $\dfrac{dv}{dt} = \dfrac{\lambda}{v}$

$\Rightarrow \displaystyle\int v\,dv = \int \lambda\,dt$

$\dfrac{v^2}{2} = \lambda t + C$

$v = u$ when $t = 0$

$\Rightarrow \dfrac{u^2}{2} = C \Rightarrow \dfrac{v^2}{2} = \lambda t + \dfrac{u^2}{2}$

When $t = T,\ v = 2u$

$\Rightarrow \dfrac{4u^2}{2} = \lambda T + \dfrac{u^2}{2}$

$\dfrac{3u^2}{2} = \lambda T$

$\Rightarrow 2\lambda T = 3u^2$

(b) $v\dfrac{dv}{dx} = \dfrac{\lambda}{v} \Rightarrow \displaystyle\int v^2\,dv = \int \lambda\,dx$

$\dfrac{v^3}{3} = \lambda x + C$

$x = 0,\ v = u$

$\Rightarrow \dfrac{u^3}{3} = C \Rightarrow \dfrac{v^3}{3} = \lambda x + \dfrac{u^3}{3}$

When $v = 2u,\quad \dfrac{8u^3}{3} = \lambda x + \dfrac{u^3}{3}$

$\Rightarrow \lambda x = \dfrac{7u^3}{3} \Rightarrow x = \dfrac{7u^3}{3\lambda}$

(c) At B, $x = 2\left(\dfrac{7u^3}{3\lambda}\right) = \dfrac{14u^3}{3\lambda}$

$\Rightarrow \dfrac{v^3}{3} = \lambda \left(\dfrac{14u^3}{3\lambda}\right) + \dfrac{u^3}{3}$

$\Rightarrow v^3 = 14u^3 + u^3 = 15u^3$

$\Rightarrow v = u\sqrt[3]{15}$

12 The forces acting on the particle are the resistance and gravity.

$F = g - 2v$: taking g to be 10 m s^{-2} gives

$F = ma = 1\dfrac{dv}{dt} = 10 - 2v = 2(5 - v)$

$\Rightarrow \left(\dfrac{1}{5-v}\right)\dfrac{dv}{dt} = 2$

Rearranging,

$\displaystyle\int \dfrac{1}{5-v}\,dv = \int 2\,dt$

$-\ln \mid 5 - v \mid\ = 2t + C$

$v = 0$ when $t = 0$

$\Rightarrow -\ln 5 = C$

$\Rightarrow -\ln \mid 5 - v \mid\ = 2t - \ln 5$

When $t = 1, -\ln \mid 5 - v \mid\ = 2 - \ln 5$

$\Rightarrow \ln 5 - \ln(5 - v) = 2$

$\ln \dfrac{5}{5-v} = 2$

Takings e's,

$\dfrac{5}{5-v} = e^2 \Rightarrow 5 - v = 5e^{-2}$

$\Rightarrow v = 5 - 5e^{-2}$

$\qquad = 5(1 - e^{-2}) = 4.32$ m s^{-1} (3 s.f.)

Section 2

1

	A	B
	3m	m
Velocity before	u	−u
Velocity after	v_A	v_B

Momentum: $3mu - mu = 3mv_A + mv_B$

$$3v_A + v_B = 2u \qquad \dots \text{①}$$

Restitution: $\dfrac{v_B - v_A}{u - (-u)} = 1$

$$v_B - v_A = 2u \qquad \dots \text{②}$$

$$\Rightarrow \quad v_A = 0, \ v_B = 2u$$

2 We can call the first sphere A, the second B and take A's initial direction of motion as positive:

$$A \longrightarrow B$$
$$\text{+ve}$$

	3m	m
Velocity before	4u	−u
Velocity after	v_A	v_B

Note that B has a negative velocity since it's moving in the opposite direction to A.

Our two equations for the collision are

Momentum: $3m \times 4u + m \times (-u)$

$$= 3mv_A + mv_B$$

i.e. $3v_A + v_B = 11u \qquad \dots \text{①}$

Restitution: $\dfrac{v_B - v_A}{4u - (-u)} = e = \frac{1}{5}$ (given)

i.e. $v_B - v_A = u \qquad \dots \text{②}$

Note that the relative speed before is $5u$ and not $3u$.

Subtracting ② from ①,

$$4v_A = 10u \ \Rightarrow v_A = \frac{5u}{2}$$

and putting this into ②

$$v_B - \frac{5u}{2} = u \ \Rightarrow v_B = \frac{7u}{2}$$

Kinetic energy before, given by $\frac{1}{2}$ mass × (velocity)², is

$$\frac{1}{2}(3m) \times (4u)^2 + \frac{1}{2}(m) \times (-u)^2 = \frac{49mu^2}{2}$$

KE after is $\frac{1}{2}(3m) \times \left(\frac{5u}{2}\right)^2 + \frac{1}{2}(m) \times \left(\frac{7u}{2}\right)^2$

$$= \frac{75mu^2}{8} + \frac{49mu^2}{8} = \frac{124mu^2}{8} = \frac{31mu^2}{2}$$

Then the loss in kinetic energy is

$$\frac{49mu^2}{2} - \frac{31mu^2}{2} = \frac{18mu^2}{2} = 9mu^2$$

3

$$A \longrightarrow B$$
$$\text{+ve}$$

	2m	3m
Velocity before	u_A	u_B

$$e = \frac{1}{5}$$

Velocity after	u	$\dfrac{3u}{2}$

Momentum: $2mu_A + 3mu_B = 2mu + 3m\dfrac{3u}{2}$

$$2u_A + 3u_B = \frac{13u}{2} \qquad \dots \text{①}$$

Restitution: $\dfrac{\frac{3u}{2} - u}{u_A - u_B} = \frac{1}{5}$

$$\frac{u}{2} = \frac{1}{5}(u_A - u_B)$$

$$u_A - u_B = \frac{5u}{2} \qquad \dots \text{②}$$

② × 2 $\quad 2u_A - 2u_B = 5u \qquad \dots \text{③}$

① − ③ $\quad 5u_B = \dfrac{3u}{2} \Rightarrow u_B = \dfrac{3u}{10}$

Into ② $\quad u_A - \dfrac{3u}{10} = \dfrac{5u}{2}$

$$\Rightarrow \quad u_A = \frac{28u}{10} = \frac{14u}{5}$$

Momentum of A: Before $2m \times \dfrac{14u}{5} = \dfrac{28mu}{5}$

After $2mu$

Change is $2mu - \dfrac{28mu}{5} = \dfrac{-18mu}{5}$, the impulse of B on A (negative because slowed down)

Then the **magnitude** (i.e. ignoring any minus sign) is

$$\frac{18mu}{5}$$

4 (a)

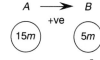

$$A \longrightarrow B$$
+ve

15m	5m

Velocity before $\quad u_A \quad\quad 0$

$e = \dfrac{1}{2}$

Velocity after $\quad v_A \quad\quad v$

Momentum: $15mu_A = 15mv_A + 5mv \quad \ldots ①$

Restitution: $\dfrac{v - v_A}{u_A} = \dfrac{1}{2} \quad\quad \ldots ②$

$① \div 5m \div \Rightarrow \quad 3v_A + v = 3u_A \quad\quad \ldots ①'$

$②$ becomes $\quad v - v_A = \dfrac{u_A}{2} \quad\quad \ldots ②'$

$②' \times 3 \quad\quad 3v - 3v_A = \dfrac{3u_A}{2} \quad\quad \ldots ③$

$①' + ③ \quad\quad 4v = 3u_A + \dfrac{3u_A}{2} = \dfrac{9u_A}{2}$

$$\Rightarrow u_A = \dfrac{8v}{9}$$

Into $②'$, $\quad v - v_A = \dfrac{4v}{9} \Rightarrow v_A = \dfrac{5v}{9}$

(b) (i) $u_A - v_A = \dfrac{3v}{9} = \dfrac{v}{3}$, so change in momentum of A is this $\times$ mass,

i.e. $15m \times \dfrac{v}{3} = 5mv$

(ii) The change in momentum of B is equal and opposite to that of A, so in magnitude $5mv$

For the next collision,

$$B \quad\quad\quad C$$

5m	λm

Velocity before $\quad v \quad\quad 0$
Velocity after $\quad v_B \quad\quad v_C$

Momentum: $5mv = 5mv_B + \lambda m v_C \quad\quad \ldots ④$

Restitution: $\dfrac{v_C - v_B}{v} = \dfrac{1}{2}$

$$\Rightarrow v_C - v_B = \dfrac{1}{2}v \quad\quad \ldots ⑤$$

$⑤ \times \lambda \quad\quad \lambda v_C - \lambda v_B = \dfrac{\lambda v}{2} \quad\quad \ldots ⑥$

$④ - ⑥ \quad\quad (5 + \lambda)v_B = 5v - \dfrac{\lambda v}{2} = v\left(5 - \dfrac{\lambda}{2}\right)$

$$\Rightarrow v_B = \dfrac{v}{5 + \lambda}\left(5 - \dfrac{\lambda}{2}\right) \quad\quad \ldots ⑦$$

If no further collisions, $v_A \le v_B$

$$\Rightarrow \dfrac{5v}{9} \le \dfrac{v}{5 + \lambda}\left(5 - \dfrac{\lambda}{2}\right)$$

$v = 0$ and $\lambda > 0$, so we can multiply through by $\dfrac{9(5 + \lambda)}{v}$

$$5(5 + \lambda) \le 9\left(5 - \dfrac{\lambda}{2}\right)$$

$$25 + 5\lambda \le 45 - \dfrac{9\lambda}{2}$$

$$5\lambda + \dfrac{9\lambda}{2} \le 45 - 25 = 20$$

$$\Rightarrow \dfrac{19\lambda}{2} \le 20 \quad \Rightarrow \quad \lambda \le \dfrac{40}{19}$$

5

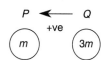

$$P \longleftarrow Q$$
+ve

m	3m

Velocity before $\quad -3u \quad\quad 6u$
Velocity after $\quad 5u \quad\quad v_Q$

Change in momentum of P is
$m(5u - (-3u)) = 8mu =$ impulse.

Since an equal and opposite impulse acts on Q, it will be $-8mu$.

With a mass of $3m$, this means that it loses $\dfrac{8mu}{3m} = \dfrac{8u}{3}$ in velocity.

$6u - \dfrac{8u}{3} = \dfrac{10u}{3}$, the speed of Q after the collision.

$$e = \dfrac{\text{Separation speed}}{\text{Approach speed}} = \dfrac{5u - \dfrac{10u}{3}}{6u + 3u} = \dfrac{\dfrac{5u}{3}}{9u}$$

$$= \dfrac{5}{27}$$

$$S \longleftarrow P$$
+ve

m	m

Velocity before $\quad 2u \quad\quad 5u$
Velocity after $\quad v_S \quad\quad v_P$

Momentum: $\quad 2mu + 5mu = mv_S + mv_P$

$$\Rightarrow v_S + v_P = 7u \quad\quad \ldots ①$$

KE before: $\frac{1}{2}m(2u)^2 + \frac{1}{2}m(5u)^2 = \frac{1}{2}m \times 29u^2$

KE after: $\frac{1}{2}mv_S^2 + \frac{1}{2}mv_P^2$

$\Rightarrow$ loss: $\frac{29}{2}mu^2 - \frac{1}{2}mv_S^2 - \frac{1}{2}mv_P^2 = 2mu^2$

$\Rightarrow \qquad v_S^2 + v_P^2 = 25u^2 \qquad \ldots ②$

Rearrange ① $\Rightarrow v_S = 7u - v_P$

into ② $(7u - v_P)^2 + v_P^2 = 25u^2$

$\qquad 49u^2 - 14v_P u + v_P^2 + v_P^2 = 25u^2$

$\qquad 2v_P^2 - 14v_P u + 24u^2 = 0$

$\qquad v_P^2 - 7v_P u + 12u^2 = 0$

$\qquad v_P = 3u \quad \text{or} \quad v_P = 4u$

$\qquad v_S = 4u \quad \text{or} \quad v_S = 3u$

But $\qquad v_S > v_P \Rightarrow v_P = 3u$

6

+ve →

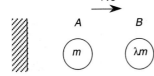

	A	B
	m	λm
Velocity before	u	0
Velocity after	v_A	v_B

By conservation of momentum:

$\qquad mu = mv_A + \lambda mv_B \qquad \ldots ①$

By Newton's Experimental Law:

$\qquad \dfrac{v_B - v_A}{u} = e = \frac{3}{5} \text{(given)} \qquad \ldots ②$

These become: $v_A + \lambda v_B = u \qquad \ldots ①'$

and $\qquad v_B - v_A = \dfrac{3u}{5} \qquad \ldots ②'$

Adding these $\quad v_B(1 + \lambda) = \dfrac{8u}{5}$

i.e. $\qquad v_B = \dfrac{8u}{5(1 + \lambda)} \qquad \ldots ③$

and putting this into ②

$\qquad \dfrac{8u}{5(1 + \lambda)} - v_A = \dfrac{3u}{5}$

$v_A = \dfrac{8u}{5(1 + \lambda)} - \dfrac{3u}{5} = \dfrac{u}{5}\left[\dfrac{8}{1 + \lambda} - 3\right]$

$\qquad = \dfrac{u}{5}\left[\dfrac{8 - 3(1 + \lambda)}{1 + \lambda}\right] = \dfrac{u}{5}\left[\dfrac{5 - 3\lambda}{1 + \lambda}\right] \qquad \ldots ④$

If the direction of v_A is to be reversed, we need this last expression for v_A to be negative, i.e.

$$\frac{u}{5}\left[\frac{5 - 3\lambda}{1 + \lambda}\right] < 0$$

since u and λ are positive, this is the same as

$$5 - 3\lambda < 0 \Rightarrow \lambda > \frac{5}{3} \text{ as required}$$

After collision with the wall, the new velocity of A, which we can call v_A^1, will be $-ev_A$, i.e.

$$v_A^1 = \frac{-e}{5}\left[u\left(\frac{5 - 3\lambda}{1 + \lambda}\right)\right]$$

$$= \frac{3u}{25}\left(\frac{3\lambda - 5}{\lambda + 1}\right)$$

reversing and substituting $e = \frac{3}{5}$.

If this velocity is greater than v_B, sphere A will catch up with sphere B, i.e. if

$$\frac{3u}{25}\left(\frac{3\lambda - 5}{\lambda + 1}\right) > \frac{8u}{5(\lambda + 1)} \text{(from ③)}$$

(we can cancel since u and $\lambda + 1$ are greater than zero)

$$\tfrac{3}{5}(3\lambda - 5) > 8 \Rightarrow 3(3\lambda - 5) > 40$$

$$9\lambda - 15 > 40 \Rightarrow 9\lambda > 55$$

$$\lambda > \frac{55}{9} \text{ as required.}$$

If $\lambda = 15$, $v_A^1 = \dfrac{3u}{25}\left(\dfrac{40}{16}\right) = \dfrac{3u}{10}$

and $v_B = \dfrac{8u}{5(16)} = \dfrac{u}{10}$

	A	B
	m	$15m$
Velocity before	$\dfrac{3u}{10}$	$\dfrac{u}{10}$
Velocity after	w_A	w_B

Momentum: $\dfrac{3mu}{10} + \dfrac{15mu}{10}$

$\qquad = mw_A + 15mw_B \qquad \ldots ⑤$

Restitution: $\dfrac{w_B - w_A}{\dfrac{3u}{10} - \dfrac{u}{10}} = \dfrac{3}{5}$ ... ⑥

⑥ becomes $w_B - w_A = \dfrac{3}{5}\left(\dfrac{3u}{10} - \dfrac{u}{10}\right) = \dfrac{3u}{25}$ ... ⑦

⑤ + ⑦ $16w_B = \dfrac{18u}{10} + \dfrac{3u}{25} = \dfrac{90u + 6u}{50} = \dfrac{48u}{25}$

$\Rightarrow w_B = \dfrac{3u}{25}$ this into ⑦ gives

$\dfrac{3u}{25} - w_A = \dfrac{3u}{25} \Rightarrow w_A = 0$

7

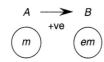

$$A \longrightarrow B$$
$$+ve$$

	m	em
Velocity before	u	eu
Velocity after	v_A	v_B

Momentum: $mu + e^2 mu$

$\qquad = mv_A + emv_B$ ... ①

Restitution: $\dfrac{v_B - v_A}{u - eu} = e$

$\Rightarrow v_B - v_A = eu(1 - e)$ ... ②

÷ ① by m $v_A + ev_B = u(1 + e^2)$ ... ③

and rearranging

Adding ② + ③

$(1 + e)v_B = eu - e^2u + u + e^2u = u(1 + e)$

$\Rightarrow v_B = u$

Putting this into ③,

$v_A + eu = u(1 + e^2)$

$\Rightarrow v_A = u(1 - e + e^2)$

To find a minimum value, we differentiate

$v_A = u(1 - e + e^2) \Rightarrow \dfrac{d\,v_A}{de} = u(-1 + 2e)$

This is zero for a minimum and since

$u \neq 0, -1 + 2e = 0$

$\Rightarrow e = \dfrac{1}{2}$

If $e = \dfrac{1}{2}$, $v_A = u\left(1 - \dfrac{1}{2} + \dfrac{1}{4}\right) = \dfrac{3u}{4}$

KE before is $\dfrac{1}{2}mu^2 + \dfrac{1}{2}(em)(eu)^2$

KE after is $\dfrac{1}{2}m\left(\dfrac{3u}{4}\right)^2 + \dfrac{1}{2}(em)(u)^2$

Total loss is

$$\left[\tfrac{1}{2}mu^2 + \tfrac{1}{2}e^3mu^2\right] - \left[\tfrac{1}{2}m\left(\tfrac{3u}{4}\right)^2 + \tfrac{1}{2}emu^2\right]$$

since $e = \dfrac{1}{2}$, this is

$$\left[\tfrac{1}{2}mu^2 + \tfrac{mu^2}{16} - \tfrac{9mu^2}{32} - \tfrac{mu^2}{4}\right] = \tfrac{mu^2}{32}$$

Momentum of A before was mu

Momentum of A after was $mu(1 - e + e^2)$

Change in momentum is

$mu - mu[1 - e + e^2] = mu[e - e^2]$

Since impulse is change in momentum, we want this to be $\dfrac{6}{25}mu$

i.e. $e - e^2 = \dfrac{6}{25} \Rightarrow 25e^2 - 25e + 6 = 0$

$\qquad (5e - 2)(5e - 3) = 0$

$\qquad \Rightarrow e = \dfrac{2}{5}$ or $e = \dfrac{3}{5}$

8

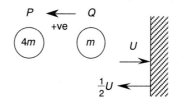

$$P \longleftarrow Q$$
$$+ve$$

$$\frac{1}{2}U \longleftarrow$$

Since the coefficient of restitution between Q and the barrier is $\dfrac{1}{2}$, it will rebound with speed $\dfrac{1}{2}U$.

KE lost is $\dfrac{1}{2}m(U^2) - \dfrac{1}{2}m\left(\dfrac{1}{2}U^2\right)$

$\qquad = \dfrac{1}{2}mU^2\left(1 - \dfrac{1}{4}\right) = \dfrac{3}{8}mU^2$

The momentum of Q just before it collides with P is $\dfrac{1}{2}mU$.

Then $4mv_P + mv_Q = \dfrac{1}{2}mU$ ... ①
   (momentum)

$\dfrac{v_P - v_Q}{\dfrac{1}{2}U} = \dfrac{2}{3} \Rightarrow v_P - v_Q = \dfrac{1}{3}U$ ... ②

   (restitution)

Dividing ① by m and adding,

$5v_P = \dfrac{5U}{6} \Rightarrow v_P = \dfrac{U}{6}$

Into ②, $\dfrac{U}{6} - v_Q = \dfrac{U}{3}$

$$\Rightarrow v_Q = \frac{U}{6} - \frac{U}{3} = -\frac{U}{6}$$

i.e. Q rebounds towards the wall. After the third collision, its velocity will be

$$\frac{1}{2} \times \frac{U}{6} = \frac{U}{12}.$$

This is not enough to catch up with P (velocity $\frac{U}{6}$), so there are three collisions altogether.

Before 2nd collision, KE is $\frac{1}{2} m \left(\frac{1}{2} U\right)^2$

After 2nd collision, KE is

$$\frac{1}{2} \times 4m \times \left(\frac{1}{6} U\right)^2 + \frac{1}{2} \times m \times \left(-\frac{1}{6} U\right)^2$$

Loss is

$$\frac{mU^2}{8} - \frac{mU^2}{18} - \frac{mU^2}{72} = \frac{mU^2}{72} [9 - 4 - 1]$$

$$= \frac{mU^2}{18}$$

Momentum of Q before was $\frac{1}{2} mU$

And after was $-\frac{1}{6} mU$ so change in momentum

$$= \frac{1}{2} mU - \left(-\frac{1}{6} mU\right) = \frac{2}{3} mU$$

$=$ the impulse on Q

9

Just before ceiling, with

$$u = U$$

$$a = -g \Rightarrow v^2 = U^2 - gh$$

$$s = \frac{h}{2} \Rightarrow v = \sqrt{U^2 - gh}$$

After impact with ceiling, $v = \frac{1}{2}\sqrt{U^2 - gh}$ downwards

$$v = V, \quad a = g, \quad s = h$$

$$\Rightarrow V^2 = \frac{1}{4}(U^2 - gh) + 2gh = \frac{U^2}{4} + \frac{7gh}{4} \quad \dots \text{①}$$

After impact with floor, $v = \frac{1}{2}\sqrt{\frac{U^2}{4} + \frac{7gh}{4}}$

$$v = 0, \quad s = h, \quad a = -g$$

$$0 = \frac{1}{4}\left(\frac{U^2}{4} + \frac{7gh}{4}\right) - 2gh$$

$$8gh = \frac{U^2}{4} + \frac{7gh}{4} \Rightarrow \frac{U^2}{4} = \frac{25gh}{4}$$

$$\Rightarrow U = 5\sqrt{gh}$$

Into ①, $V^2 = \frac{25gh}{4} + \frac{7gh}{4} = \frac{32gh}{4} = 8gh$

$$\Rightarrow V = \sqrt{8gh}$$

Just before ceiling, $v = -\sqrt{25gh - gh}$

$$= -\sqrt{24gh}$$

Just after, $v = +\frac{1}{2}\sqrt{24gh}$

$$\Rightarrow \text{impulse is } \frac{3}{2} m \sqrt{24gh}$$

Just before floor, $v = \sqrt{8gh}$

Just after, $v = -\frac{1}{2}\sqrt{8gh}$

$$\Rightarrow \text{impulse is } \frac{3}{2} m \sqrt{8gh}$$

$\Rightarrow$ ratio ceiling : floor is

$$\frac{3}{2} m \sqrt{24gh} : \frac{3}{2} m \sqrt{8gh} \Rightarrow \sqrt{3} : 1$$

Section 3

1 In equilibrium $T = mg$ and also, for an

elastic string, $T = \dfrac{\lambda x}{l}$. Equating these with

$m = 2$, $l = 3$ and $\lambda = 12g$ gives

$$mg = \frac{\lambda x}{l} \Rightarrow 2g = \frac{12gx}{3}$$

$$\Rightarrow x = 0.5 \text{ m}$$

2 As before, $mg = \dfrac{\lambda x}{l}$ with $m = 0.5$ (in kg)

$l = 0.5$ $x = 0.05$

$$\Rightarrow 0.5g = \frac{\lambda\, 0.05}{0.5} \Rightarrow \lambda = 5g$$

3

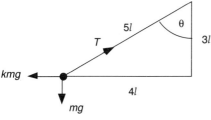

Marking in the angle θ and noting that the triangle is $3 - 4 - 5$ so that

$\sin \theta = \dfrac{4}{5}$, $\cos \theta = \dfrac{3}{5}$, $\tan \theta = \dfrac{4}{3}$

Resolving vertically, $T \cos \theta = mg$ ... ①

   horizontally, $T \sin \theta = kmg$ ... ②

But the string is elastic with the extension $x = 5l - 4l = l$, and so

$$T = \frac{\lambda\,(\text{extension})}{\text{natural length}} = \frac{\lambda l}{4l} = \frac{\lambda}{4}$$

Putting this into ① with $\cos \theta = \dfrac{3}{5}$ gives

$$\frac{\lambda}{4} \times \frac{3}{5} = mg \Rightarrow \lambda = \frac{20mg}{3}$$

Hence $T = \dfrac{\lambda}{4} = \dfrac{\frac{20mg}{3}}{4} = \dfrac{5mg}{3}$

Dividing equation ② by ① gives

$$\frac{T \sin \theta}{T \cos \theta} = \frac{kmg}{mg} \Rightarrow k = \tan \theta = \frac{4}{3}$$

4 The tension throughout the joined string will be the same and since the suspended particle has mass M, this tension will be Mg.

For AB: $T = \dfrac{\lambda_1 x_1}{c} \Rightarrow Mg = \dfrac{9Mg\, x_1}{c}$

$$\Rightarrow x_1 = \frac{c}{9} \qquad \text{... ①}$$

For CD: $T = \dfrac{\lambda_2 x_2}{c} \Rightarrow Mg = \dfrac{12Mg\, x_2}{c}$

$$\Rightarrow x_2 = \frac{c}{12} \qquad \text{... ②}$$

The length of AD will be:

natural lengths + total extension

i.e. $c + c + \dfrac{c}{9} + \dfrac{c}{12} = \dfrac{79c}{36}$

5

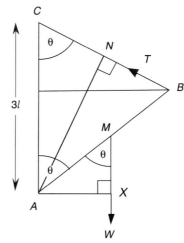

Mark in $A\hat{C}B$ as θ.

Since $AB = BC$, $C\hat{A}B = \theta$.

Since AC parallel to MX, $A\hat{M}X = \theta$

Taking moments about A,

$T \times (AN) - W \times (AX) = 0$ ... ①

From $\triangle ACN$, $AN = AC \sin \theta$

$= 3l \sin \theta$ ... ②

From $\triangle AMX$, since M is the midpoint of AB, $AM = 2l$

and $AX = AM \sin \theta$

$= 2l \sin \theta$ ... ③

Putting ② and ③ into ① ,

$$T \times 3l \sin\theta - W \times 2l \sin\theta = 0$$

$$T = W \times \frac{2l \sin\theta}{3l \sin\theta} = \frac{2W}{3}$$

Since $BC = AB = 4l$, the extension is l

$$T = \frac{\lambda \text{ extension}}{\text{natural length}} = \frac{\lambda l}{3l} \Rightarrow \lambda = 3T = 2W$$

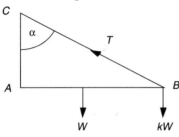

$$\text{Sin } \alpha = \frac{4}{5}$$

ΔABC is now $3 - 4 - 5$, with $BC = 5l$. The extension in the string is now $2l$, and so

$$T = \frac{2W \times 2l}{3l} = \frac{4W}{3}$$

Moments about A:

$$W \times 2l + kW \times 4l - T \times 3l \sin\theta = 0$$

$$2lW + 4klW = \frac{4W}{3} \times 3l \times \frac{4}{5}$$

$$4kW = \frac{16W}{5} - 2W = \frac{6W}{5} \Rightarrow k = \frac{3}{10}$$

6 (a)

$$A \xmapsto{\hspace{2cm}} B$$
$$\xleftarrow{\quad 0.6 \text{ m} \quad}$$

If the natural length is l, the extension is $0.6 - l$

Using $T = \frac{\lambda x}{l} \Rightarrow 3 = \frac{\lambda \times (0.6 - l)}{l}$ ... ①

(b) Using $EE = \frac{\lambda x^2}{2l}$,

and the new extension $x = 0.7 - l$

$$\Rightarrow 0.6 = \frac{\lambda \times (0.7 - l)^2}{2l}$$ ... ②

Dividing ① by ②, $\dfrac{3}{0.6} = \dfrac{0.6 - l}{\dfrac{(0.7 - l)^2}{2}}$

$$\Rightarrow \frac{5}{2}(0.7 - l)^2 = 0.6 - l$$

$$\Rightarrow \frac{5}{2}(0.49 - 1.4l + l^2) = 0.6 - l$$

$$\Rightarrow 2.45 - 7l + 5l^2 = 1.2 - 2l$$

$$\Rightarrow 5l^2 - 5l + 1.25 = 0$$

$$\Rightarrow l^2 - l + \frac{1}{4} = 0 \Rightarrow (l - \tfrac{1}{2})^2 = 0 \Rightarrow l = 0.5$$

Putting this into ① gives $3 = \dfrac{\lambda(0.1)}{0.5}$

$$\Rightarrow \lambda = 15$$

7

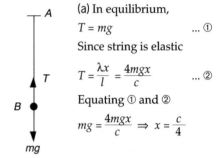

(a) In equilibrium,

$$T = mg$$ ... ①

Since string is elastic

$$T = \frac{\lambda x}{l} = \frac{4mgx}{c}$$ ... ②

Equating ① and ②

$$mg = \frac{4mgx}{c} \Rightarrow x = \frac{c}{4}$$

(b) At A, KE is zero

PE is zero (taking level of A as zero level)

EE is zero

At D, the point of maximum distance between A and B, which we can call d,

KE is zero (since at rest before going up again)

PE is $-mgd$ (negative since a loss)

EE is $\dfrac{\lambda(d - c)^2}{2c}$ since $d = c + x$, when x is the extension

$$\Rightarrow x = d - c$$

i.e. $\dfrac{\lambda(d - c)^2}{2c} = mgd \Rightarrow \dfrac{4mg(d - c)^2}{2c} = mgd$

$$4(d - c)^2 = 2cd \Rightarrow 2d^2 - 4cd + 2c^2 = cd$$

$$2d^2 - 5cd + 2c^2 = 0$$

$$(2d - c)(d - 2c) = 0$$

Since $d > c$, we ignore $d = \dfrac{c}{2}$,

and then $d = 2c$

8　$T = mg = \dfrac{\lambda x}{l} = \dfrac{\lambda \times \frac{l}{12}}{l} \Rightarrow \lambda = 12mg$

At top, PE = 0 = EE

At greatest depth, PE = $-mgd$

$EE = \dfrac{1}{2}\dfrac{\lambda x^2}{l} = \dfrac{1}{2} \times \dfrac{12mg \times (d-l)^2}{l}$

$\Rightarrow -mgd + \dfrac{6mg(d-l)^2}{l} = 0$

$\Rightarrow -dl + 6d^2 - 12dl + 6l^2 = 0$

$\Rightarrow 6d^2 - 13dl + 6l^2 = 0$

$\Rightarrow (3d - 2l)(2d - 3l) = 0$

$\Rightarrow d = \dfrac{2l}{3}$, not possible, or $d = \dfrac{3l}{2}$

$\Rightarrow$ extension is $\dfrac{l}{2}$

When it has fallen a distance h,

$PE = -mgh \quad KE = \dfrac{1}{2}mv^2$

$EE = \dfrac{1}{2} \times \dfrac{12mg \times (h-l)^2}{l}$

These add up to zero, so

$K = \dfrac{1}{2}mv^2 = mgh - \dfrac{6mg\,(h-l)^2}{l}$

To find maximum, differentiate both sides with respect to the variable h and put

$\dfrac{dK}{dh} = 0$

i.e. $mg - \dfrac{12mg\,(h-l)}{l} = 0$

$\Rightarrow 12(h - l) = l$

$12h - 12l = l$

$h = \dfrac{13l}{12}$, i.e. equilibrium position

9　The acceleration will be zero when no force is acting, i.e. at the static equilibrium position.

$T = \dfrac{\lambda x}{l} \Rightarrow mg = \dfrac{3mgx}{a} \Rightarrow x = \dfrac{a}{3}$

Distance AP is $a + \dfrac{a}{3} = \dfrac{4a}{3}$

Maximum speed is when acceleration is zero, i.e. when $x = \dfrac{a}{3}$

At top, PE = 0 (zero level)

$KE = \dfrac{1}{2}m\,(\sqrt{3ga}\,)^2 = \dfrac{3mga}{2}$

EE = 0

When $x = \dfrac{a}{3} \quad PE = -\dfrac{4mga}{3}$

$KE = \dfrac{1}{2}mv^2$

$EE = \dfrac{1}{2} \times \dfrac{3mg\,(\frac{a}{3})^2}{a} = \dfrac{mga}{6}$

Equating the two sums,

$\dfrac{3mga}{2} = -\dfrac{4mga}{3} + \dfrac{1}{2}mv^2 + \dfrac{mga}{6}$

$\dfrac{3mga}{2} + \dfrac{4mga}{3} - \dfrac{mga}{6} = \dfrac{1}{2}mv^2$

$\dfrac{1}{2}v^2 = \dfrac{16ga}{6} \Rightarrow v = 4\sqrt{\dfrac{ga}{3}}$ (maximum)

10

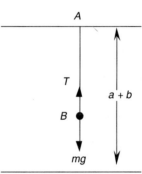

(a) In equilibrium, $T = mg$ 　　　　... ①

but $\quad T = \dfrac{\lambda x}{l} = \dfrac{mga}{b} \times \dfrac{x}{a}$ 　　　... ②

Equating ① and ②, $mg = \dfrac{mgx}{b} \Rightarrow x = b$

and so AB is $a + b$, the ball is just in contact with the floor.

(b) The sum of the energies at A will be $mg(a + b)$, the potential energy (taking the floor to be the zero level). Just before striking the floor, the kinetic energy will be $\dfrac{1}{2}mv^2$ and the elastic energy

$\dfrac{1}{2}\lambda\dfrac{x^2}{l} = \dfrac{1}{2} \times \dfrac{mga}{b} \times \dfrac{b^2}{a} = \dfrac{mgb}{2}$

with sum $\dfrac{1}{2}mv^2 + \dfrac{mgb}{2}$

Equating these two sums,

$$mg(a + b) = \frac{1}{2}mv^2 + \frac{mgb}{2}$$

$$mga + mgb = \frac{1}{2}mv^2 + \frac{mgb}{2}$$

$$\Rightarrow \frac{1}{2}mv^2 = mga + \frac{mgb}{2}$$

$$v^2 = 2ga + gb = g(2a + b)$$

If the coefficient of restitution is e, the velocity after bouncing will be $ev = e\sqrt{g(2a + b)}$. This represents a kinetic energy of $\frac{1}{2}mv^2 = \frac{1}{2}me^2\left[g(2a + b)\right]$

The potential energy at the maximum height a after rebound is mga.

Equating these two energies,

$$\frac{1}{2}me^2\left[g(2a + b)\right] = mga$$

$$e^2(2a + b) = 2a$$

$$\Rightarrow e^2 = \frac{2a}{2a + b}$$

$$\Rightarrow e = \sqrt{\frac{2a}{2a + b}}$$

11

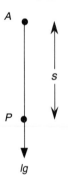

(a) When s, the distance fallen, is less than or equal to 0.5 m, the natural length of the string, there will be no elastic energy stored in the string and so we have simply that

Gain in kinetic energy = Loss in potential energy

i.e. $\frac{1}{2}mv^2 = mgs$

$$\Rightarrow v^2 = 2gs$$

(b) When $s > 0.5$, there will be an extension of $s - 0.5$ m, and so the stored elastic energy will be

$$\frac{1}{2}\lambda\frac{x^2}{l} = \frac{1}{2} \times 40 \times \frac{(s - 0.5^2)}{0.5} = 40(s - 0.5)^2$$

The kinetic energy will be $\frac{1}{2}mv^2$ and taking the level of A as our zero potential level, there will be a loss of potential energy of magnitude mgs. Since the sum of the energies at A was zero, the sum of these three energies will also be zero, i.e.

$$40(s - 0.5)^2 + \frac{1}{2}mv^2 - mgs = 0$$

Put $m = 1$ and rearrange, $g = 10$

$$\frac{1}{2}v^2 = 10s - 40(s^2 - s + 0.25)$$

$$= 10s - 40s^2 + 40s - 10$$

$$v^2 = 100s - 80s^2 - 20 \qquad \ldots \text{①}$$

At maximum speed, $\frac{dv}{ds} = 0$.
Differentiating ① with respect to s,

$$2v\frac{dv}{ds} = 100 - 160s$$

If $\frac{dv}{ds} = 0$, then $100 - 160s = 0 \Rightarrow s = \frac{5}{8}$ m

For maximum distance, $v = 0$,

i.e. $100s - 80s^2 - 20 = 0$

$\div 20$ and rearrange:

$$4s^2 - 5s + 1 = 0$$

$$(4s - 1)(s - 1) = 0 \Rightarrow s = \frac{1}{4} \text{ or } s = 1 \text{ m}$$

(Discard $s = \frac{1}{4}$ since we're considering $s > 0.5$)

If $v = 2.5$, $v^2 = 6.25$ and putting this into ①

$$6.25 = 100s - 80s^2 - 20$$

$$80s^2 - 100s + 26.25 = 0 \qquad \times 4$$

$$320s^2 - 400s + 105 = 0 \qquad \div 5$$

$$64s^2 - 80s + 21 = 0$$

$$(8s - 3)(8s - 7) = 0$$

then $s = \frac{3}{8}$

(i.e. before the string is stretched)

and $s = \frac{7}{8}$

12 PE = work done = $\int_0^x T \, dx = \frac{\lambda x^2}{2a}$

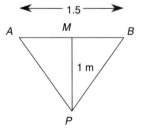

$\triangle AMP$ is right-angled, $3 - 4 - 5$,
so that $AP = 1.25$ m
i.e. AP is extended 0.5 m.
BP has a similar extension.

At M:

KE = 0 PE = 0 (zero level) EE = 0

Depth 1: $KE = \dfrac{1}{2} mv^2$ $PE = - mg$

$$EE = \left[\frac{1}{2} \, \frac{48 \times (0.5)^2}{0.75} \right] \times 2$$

$$\Rightarrow \frac{1}{2} mv^2 = mg - \frac{48 \times (0.5)^2}{0.75}$$

$$\Rightarrow v^2 = 2g - 16 = 4 \Rightarrow v = 2 \text{ m s}^{-1}$$

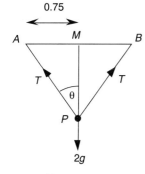

In equilibrium, $2T \cos \theta = 2g$ ... ①

$AP = \dfrac{0.75}{\sin \theta} \Rightarrow$ extension $x = AP - 0.75$

$$= 0.75 \left(\frac{1}{\sin \theta} - 1 \right) \quad \text{... ②}$$

Using $T = \dfrac{\lambda x}{a}$

$$\Rightarrow T = \frac{48}{0.75} (0.75) \left(\frac{1}{\sin \theta} - 1 \right)$$

$$= 48 \left(\frac{1}{\sin \theta} - 1 \right)$$

Into ① gives $48 \left(\dfrac{\cos \theta}{\sin \theta} - \cos \theta \right) = 10$

$$\Rightarrow \cot \theta - \cos \theta = \frac{5}{24}$$

13 Originally the extension was $(1.2 - 1) = 0.2$ and so stored energy was

$$T = \frac{\lambda x^2}{2l} = \frac{12(0.2)^2}{2} = 0.24 \text{ J}$$

Dropping 0.5 gives a $5 - 12 - 13$ $\triangle$, with $OB = 1.3 \Rightarrow$ extension of 0.3.

New stored energy is

$$\frac{12(0.3)^2}{2} = 0.54 \text{ J}$$

Increase is 0.3 J.

It has lost $mgh = 0.1 \times 10 \times 0.5 = 0.5$ J

Gain in KE is 0.2 J $= \dfrac{1}{2} mv^2$

$$\Rightarrow v^2 = 4 \Rightarrow v = 2$$

14 Basically, the inital KE is converted to stored elastic energy.

KE initial is $\dfrac{1}{2} mv^2 = \dfrac{1}{2} m (2ga) = mga$

If x is the subsequent compression, stored energy is

$$\frac{1}{2} \frac{\lambda x^2}{l} = \frac{1}{2} \times \frac{6mg \times x^2}{3a} \Rightarrow x = a$$

Equating these, $mga = \dfrac{mgx^2}{a} \Rightarrow x = a$

Section 4

1. (a) 2π rad s^{-1} (b) $10\pi^2$ rad s^{-1}

2. (a) 0.5 rev s^{-1} (b) $\dfrac{5}{2\pi}$ rev s^{-1}

3. (a) $\dfrac{1}{4}$ second   (b) $\dfrac{2\pi}{3}$ seconds
   (c) 0.5 second   (d) 4π seconds
   (e) $\dfrac{20}{7}$ seconds

4. $F = \dfrac{mv^2}{r} \Rightarrow 4.8 = \dfrac{3 \times 16}{r} \Rightarrow r = \dfrac{48}{4.8} = 10$ m

5. 3 rev s$^{-1} \equiv 3 \times 2\pi$ rad s$^{-1} = \omega$
   $F = mr\omega^2 = 2 \times 0.5 \times (6\pi)^2$
   $= 36\pi^2$ N $(= 355.3$ N$)$

6.

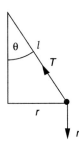

$\tan \theta = \dfrac{5}{12}$

$\Rightarrow \sin \theta = \dfrac{5}{13}$

and $\cos \theta = \dfrac{12}{13}$

Vertically: $T \cos \theta = mg$ ... ①

Horizontally: $T \sin \theta = m\dfrac{v^2}{r}$ ... ②

Δ : $\sin \theta = \dfrac{r}{l}$ ... ③

Dividing ② by ①, $\dfrac{T \sin \theta}{T \cos \theta} = \dfrac{\dfrac{mv^2}{r}}{mg}$

$\Rightarrow \tan \theta = \dfrac{v^2}{rg} = \dfrac{5}{12}$ (given)

i.e. $r = \dfrac{12v^2}{5g} = \dfrac{12(2)^2}{5g} = \dfrac{48}{5g}$ ... ④

Also from Δ, $\sin \theta = \dfrac{r}{l}$ but $\sin \theta = \dfrac{5}{13}$

$\Rightarrow r = \dfrac{5l}{13}$ ... ⑤

Equating ④ and ⑤, $\dfrac{48}{5g} = \dfrac{5l}{13}$

$\Rightarrow l = \dfrac{48 \times 13}{25g} \approx 2.5$m if g is 10 m s^{-2}

7.

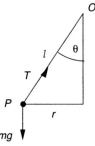

Suppose the mass of the particle is m.

Vertically: $T \cos \theta - mg = 0$ ... ①

Horizontally: $T \sin \theta = mr\omega^2$ ... ②

Δ: $\sin \theta = \dfrac{r}{l}$ ... ③

Rearrange ① to get $T \cos \theta = mg$ and divide ② by this

$\dfrac{T \sin \theta}{T \cos \theta} = \dfrac{mr\omega^2}{mg}$

i.e. $\sin \theta = \dfrac{r\omega^2 \cos \theta}{g}$ ... ④

Putting ③ and ④ together

$\dfrac{r}{l} = \dfrac{r\omega^2 \cos \theta}{g}$

$\Rightarrow \cos \theta = \dfrac{g}{l\omega^2}$ ... ⑤

Now we're told that the particle makes 2 revolutions in one second, i.e.

$2 \times 2\pi = 4\pi$ rad s^{-1} or $\omega = 4\pi$.

Substituting this into ⑤,

$\cos \theta = \dfrac{g}{l \times 16\pi^2}$ and since $l = 0.125 = \dfrac{1}{8}$,

$\cos \theta = \dfrac{8g}{16\pi^2} = \dfrac{g}{2\pi^2}$

8

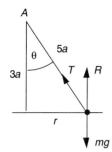

Vertically: $R + T \cos \theta = mg$ ... ①

Horizontally: $T \sin \theta = mr\omega^2$ ... ②

Δ: $\cos \theta = \dfrac{3}{5} \Rightarrow r = 4a$

(a) $R = 0$, from ①, $T_1 \cos \theta = mg$

$\Rightarrow T_1 = \dfrac{mg}{\cos \theta} = \dfrac{5mg}{3}$

(b) $R = \dfrac{3mg}{4}$, from ①,

$T_2 \cos \theta = mg - \dfrac{3mg}{4} = \dfrac{mg}{4}$

$T_2 = \dfrac{5mg}{12}$

Since from ②, $\omega^2 = \dfrac{T \sin \theta}{mr} = kT$

where $k = \dfrac{\sin \theta}{mr}$, constant

(a) When T_1, $\omega_1^2 = k\dfrac{5mg}{3}$

(b) When T_2, $\omega_2^2 = k\dfrac{5mg}{12}$

then $\dfrac{\omega_1^2}{\omega_2^2} = 4 \Rightarrow \dfrac{\omega_1}{\omega_2} = 2$

ω_1 is twice as fast as ω_2, so the times for one revolution will be $1 : 2$.

9

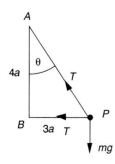

Vertically: $T \cos \theta = mg$ ... ①

Δ: $\tan \theta = \dfrac{3}{4} \Rightarrow \cos \theta = \dfrac{4}{5}$ ... ②

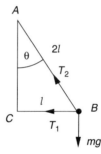

$\sin \theta = \dfrac{3}{5}$

Then from ① and ②, $T \times \dfrac{4}{5} = mg$

$\Rightarrow T = \dfrac{5mg}{4}$

Horizontally: $T + T \sin \theta = \dfrac{mv^2}{r}$

$\dfrac{5mg}{4} + \dfrac{5mg}{4} \times \dfrac{3}{5} = \dfrac{mv^2}{3a}$

$2mg = \dfrac{mv^2}{3a} \Rightarrow v^2 = 6ga$

10

Vertically: $T_2 \cos \theta = mg$ ... ①

Δ: $\sin \theta = \dfrac{l}{2l} = \dfrac{1}{2} \Rightarrow \theta = 30°$ ... ②

This into ① gives $T_2 \cos 30° = mg$

$\Rightarrow T_2 = \dfrac{2mg}{\sqrt{3}} \quad \left(= \dfrac{2mg\sqrt{3}}{3} \right)$

Horizontally: $T_1 + T_2 \sin \theta = \dfrac{mu^2}{l}$ ... ③

$T_1 + T_2 \times \dfrac{1}{2} = \dfrac{mu^2}{l}$

$T_1 = \dfrac{mu^2}{l} - \dfrac{T_2}{2} = \dfrac{mu^2}{l} - \dfrac{mg}{\sqrt{3}}$

Motion is only possible when $T_1 \geq 0$, i.e.

$\dfrac{mu^2}{l} - \dfrac{mg}{\sqrt{3}} \geq 0 \qquad \dfrac{mu^2}{l} \geq \dfrac{mg}{\sqrt{3}}$

$u^2 \geq \dfrac{gl}{\sqrt{3}} = \dfrac{gl\sqrt{3}}{3}$

11

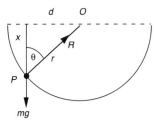

Since the bowl is smooth, the reaction on the particle will be perpendicular to the tangent at that point, i.e. it will pass through the centre of the circle. Call this reaction R and the angle θ and length d as marked in the diagram.

Vertically: $R \cos \theta - mg = 0$ ... ①

Horizontally: $R \sin \theta = \dfrac{mv^2}{d}$ ... ②

Δ: $r^2 = x^2 + d^2$ ... ③

$\tan \theta = \dfrac{d}{x}$ ... ④

Rearranging ①, $R \cos \theta = mg$

and dividing ② by this gives

$\dfrac{R \sin \theta}{R \cos \theta} = \dfrac{\frac{mv^2}{d}}{mg} \Rightarrow \tan \theta = \dfrac{v^2}{gd}$ ... ⑤

Combining this with ④, $\dfrac{d}{x} = \dfrac{v^2}{gd}$

$\Rightarrow v^2 = \dfrac{gd^2}{x}$

But from ③, $d^2 = r^2 - x^2$

$\Rightarrow v^2 = g\left(\dfrac{r^2 - x^2}{x}\right)$

and $v = \sqrt{\dfrac{g(r^2 - x^2)}{x}}$

From ①, $R = \dfrac{mg}{\cos \theta}$

and since, from the triangle, $\cos \theta = \dfrac{x}{r}$,

$R = \dfrac{mg}{\frac{x}{r}} \Rightarrow R = \dfrac{mgr}{x}$

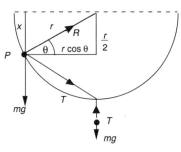

Since $\sin \theta = \dfrac{\frac{r}{2}}{r} = \dfrac{1}{2}$, $\theta = 30°$ and the tension will also be at this angle, but below the horizontal.

Vertically: $R \sin 30° = mg + T \sin 30°$ ... ①

Horizontally: $R \cos 30° + T \cos 30°$

$= \dfrac{mv^2}{r \cos 30°}$ ... ②

Since we're given that $T = mg$, putting in the trig. ratios these equations become

$\dfrac{R}{2} = mg + \dfrac{mg}{2} = \dfrac{3mg}{2} \Rightarrow R = 3mg$ ... ③

and so this value into ②,

$3mg \times \dfrac{\sqrt{3}}{2} + mg \times \dfrac{\sqrt{3}}{2} = \dfrac{mv^2}{r \times \dfrac{\sqrt{3}}{2}}$

$\times \dfrac{r\sqrt{3}}{2}$ $v^2 = \dfrac{9gr}{4} + \dfrac{3gr}{4} = \dfrac{12gr}{4} = 3rg$

12

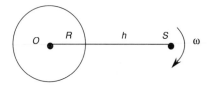

We're given an acceleration (rather than a force) which is $\dfrac{k}{r^2}$. On the surface of the earth, i.e. when $r = R$, this is g,

i.e. $\dfrac{k}{R^2} = g \Rightarrow k = gR^2$

and so the acceleration is $\dfrac{gR^2}{r^2}$ ... ①

This acceleration is the acceleration of the satellite towards the centre of the earth, i.e. $r\omega^2$ and so

$\dfrac{gR^2}{r^2} = r\omega^2 \Rightarrow \omega^2 = \dfrac{gR^2}{r^3}$ ... ②

But at a height h above the surface of the earth, $r = R + h$ and ② becomes

$$\omega^2 = \frac{gR^2}{(R+h)^3}$$

i.e. $\omega = \left(\frac{gR^2}{(R+h)^3}\right)^{\frac{1}{2}}$

For the next part, we need to take care with the units!

When $R = 6400$ km

$$= 6.4 \times 10^6 \text{ m and } h = 1.6 \times 10^6 \text{ m,}$$

$$\omega = \left(\frac{g \times 6.4^2 \times 10^{12}}{8^3 \times 10^{18}}\right)^{\frac{1}{2}}$$

$$= 0.885 \times 10^{-3} \text{ rad s}^{-1}$$

$$= 5.313 \times 10^{-2} \text{ rad min}^{-1}.$$

For a complete revolution,

$$T = \frac{2\pi}{\omega} = 118 \text{ mins}$$

This is approximately 2 hours

13 Since in equilibrium, $T = mg$ and $t = \frac{\lambda x}{l}$

where $= \lambda\, 3mg,$

$$mg = \frac{3mgx}{l} \Rightarrow x = \frac{l}{3}$$

and the stretched length of the string is $\frac{4l}{3}$

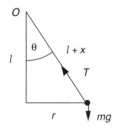

Vertically: $T \cos\theta = mg$ ... ①

Horizontally: $T \sin\theta = mr\omega^2$ ... ②

Elasticity: $T = \frac{3mgx}{l}$ ... ③

③ into ① $\Rightarrow \dfrac{3mgx}{l} \cos\theta = mg$

but $\cos\theta = \dfrac{l}{l+x}$

$$\frac{3x}{l} \times \frac{l}{l+x} = 1 \Rightarrow 3x = l + x \Rightarrow x = \frac{l}{2}$$

and so stretched length is $\dfrac{3l}{2}$.

③ into ② $\Rightarrow \dfrac{3mgx}{l} \sin\theta = mr\omega^2$

and $\sin\theta = \dfrac{r}{l+x} = \dfrac{2r}{3l}$

$$\frac{3gx}{l} \times \frac{2r}{3l} = r\omega^2 \text{ and } x = \frac{l}{2}$$

$$\frac{\frac{gl}{2}}{l} \times \frac{2}{l} = \omega^2 \Rightarrow \omega^2 l = g$$

14 In equilibrium, $T = mg = \dfrac{\lambda x}{l}$

$$\Rightarrow 5g = \frac{\lambda\, 0.025}{0.2}$$

$$\Rightarrow \lambda = \frac{g}{0.025} = 392 \text{ N}$$

(a)

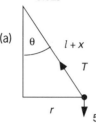

Vertically: $T \cos\theta = 5g$

and since $T = 98$ and $g = 9.8$

$$\cos\theta = \frac{5 \times 9.8}{98} = \frac{1}{2} \Rightarrow \theta = 60°$$

Elasticity: $T = \dfrac{\lambda x}{l} = \dfrac{392x}{0.2} = 98$ (given)

$$\Rightarrow x = \frac{0.2}{4} = 0.05$$

Horizontally: $T \sin\theta = mr\omega^2$

and Δ, $\sin\theta = \dfrac{r}{l+x}$

Combining $98 \times \dfrac{r}{0.25} = 5r\omega^2$

$$\Rightarrow \omega^2 = \frac{4 \times 98}{5} \Rightarrow \omega = \sqrt{\frac{392}{5}} \text{ rad s}^{-1}$$

$$= 8.9 \text{ (1 d.p.)}$$

(b) On limit, $T = 196 = \dfrac{392x}{0.2}$

$\Rightarrow x$ would be 0.1

As before, $T \sin\theta = mr\omega^2$ and $\sin\theta = \dfrac{r}{l+x}$

$$\Rightarrow T\left(\frac{r}{l+x}\right) = mr\omega^2$$

and since $T = 196$, $m = 5$ and $l + x = 0.3$

$$\frac{196}{0.3 \times 5} = \omega^2 \Rightarrow \omega = 11.4 \text{ rad s}^{-1} \text{ (1 d.p.)}$$

Section 5

1 $a = 7$

$$T = 4 \implies \frac{2\pi}{\omega} = 4 \implies \omega = \frac{2\pi}{4} = \frac{\pi}{2}$$

$$v_{\text{MAX}} = \omega a = \frac{7\pi}{2} \text{ cm s}^{-1}$$

$v^2 = \omega^2(a^2 - x^2)$ and when $x = 3$

$$v^2 = \left(\frac{\pi}{2}\right)^2 [49 - 9] = \left(\frac{\pi}{2}\right)^2 (40)$$

$$\implies v = \frac{\pi}{2}\sqrt{40} \quad = \pi\sqrt{10} \text{ cm s}^{-1}$$

2 (a) Since acceleration is $-\omega^2 x$ and we're told that it is positive $\frac{9}{4}$, the distance x must be negative, i.e. $x = -9$

$$\implies \frac{9}{4} = -\omega^2 \times (-9) \implies -\omega^2 = \frac{1}{4}, \omega = \frac{1}{2}$$

The period $T = \frac{2\pi}{\omega} = \frac{2\pi}{\frac{1}{2}} = 4\pi$ seconds

(b) $v^2 = \omega^2(a^2 - x^2) \implies 36 = \frac{1}{4}(a^2 - 81)$

$$\implies 144 = a^2 - 81$$

$$a^2 = 225 \implies a = 15 \text{ m}$$

(c) $v_{\text{MAX}} = \omega a = \frac{15}{2} \text{ m s}^{-1}$

3 (a) 5 complete oscillations per second means that time for one oscillation, T, is $\frac{1}{5}$ sec

$$\implies T = \frac{2\pi}{\omega} = \frac{1}{5} \implies \omega = 10\pi$$

Distance between extremes is twice the amplitude, so

$2a = 0.1 \implies a = 0.05$ m.

$v_{\text{MAX}} = \omega a = 10\pi \times 0.05 = \frac{\pi}{2} \text{ m s}^{-1}$.

Maximum force $\implies$ acceleration is a maximum $\implies x = a$ and magnitude is

$\omega^2 a = 100\pi^2 \times 0.05 = 5\pi^2$.

$F = ma$, so maximum force is

$0.2 \times 5\pi^2 = \pi^2 \text{ N}$

(b) Frequency is unaltered $\implies \omega = 10\pi$ still, a is now 0.1 and we want speed when $x = 0.05$

$$v^2 = \omega^2(a^2 - x^2) = 100\pi^2(0.1^2 - 0.05^2)$$

$$= 100\pi^2(0.0075)$$

$$\implies v = 2.72 \approx 2.7 \text{ m s}^{-1}$$

4

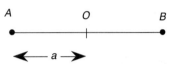

If a is the amplitude, we connect the distance and velocity by the formula

$$v^2 = \omega^2(a^2 - x^2)$$

Putting the two pairs of values for v and x into this gives

$$4^2 = \omega^2(a^2 - 4^2) \qquad \text{... ①}$$

and $8^2 = \omega^2(a^2 - 2^2) \qquad \text{... ②}$

Dividing ② by ① to eliminate the ω^2,

$$\frac{8^2}{4^2} = \frac{a^2 - 2^2}{a^2 - 4^2} \implies 4 = \frac{a^2 - 4}{a^2 - 16}$$

$$4a^2 - 64 = a^2 - 4$$

$$3a^2 = 60$$

$$a^2 = 20$$

$$a = 2\sqrt{5} \text{ m} \qquad \text{... ③}$$

Since a is *half* the distance between A and B, distance AB is $4\sqrt{5}$ m.

Substituting $a = 2\sqrt{5}$ back into ① gives

$$16 = \omega^2(20 - 16)$$

$$\implies \omega^2 = 4, \omega = 2$$

Since the *period* of the oscillation is given by $\frac{2\pi}{\omega}$, this will be $\frac{2\pi}{2} = \pi$ seconds.

When 2 m from A, it will be $(2\sqrt{5} - 2)$ m from O and its speed is given by

$$v^2 = \omega^2(a^2 - x^2)$$

$$= 4[(2\sqrt{5})^2 - (2\sqrt{5} - 2)^2] \text{ since } \omega = 2$$

$$= 4(2)(4\sqrt{5} - 2) \text{ using } a^2 - b^2 = (a - b)(a + b)$$

Since kinetic energy is $\frac{1}{2}mv^2$, this will be

$\frac{1}{2} \times 2 \times 4 \times 2(4\sqrt{5} - 2) = 16(2\sqrt{5} - 1)$ J

If M is the mid-point of OB, OM is $\frac{a}{2}$,

i.e. $x = \frac{a}{2}$.

Using the formula $\quad t = \frac{1}{\omega} \sin^{-1} \frac{x}{a}$

where the time t is measured from the point when the particle is at O,

$t = \frac{1}{2} \sin^{-1} \frac{\frac{a}{2}}{a} = \frac{1}{2} \sin^{-1} \frac{1}{2} = \frac{1}{2} \times \frac{\pi}{6} = \frac{\pi}{12}$

This is the time from O to M. For A to O, which is $\frac{1}{4}$ of an oscillation, the time is

$\frac{1}{4} \times \pi = \frac{\pi}{4}$

Total time from A to M is $\frac{\pi}{4} + \frac{\pi}{12} = \frac{\pi}{3}$

5 The maximum speed is $\omega a = 0.5$ $\qquad$ ①
The maximum acceleration is when $x = a$,
i.e. $\omega^2 a = 0.1$ $\qquad$ ②

② ÷ ① $\Rightarrow$ $\omega = 0.2$,

so the period $T = \frac{2\pi}{\omega} = \frac{2\pi}{0.2} = 10\pi$ s

The amplitude a, from ① is

$a = \frac{0.5}{\omega} = \frac{0.5}{0.2} = 2.5$ m

6 Given that $a = 4$ and $\frac{2\pi}{\omega} = 8 \Rightarrow \omega = \frac{2\pi}{8} = \frac{\pi}{4}$

(a) Maximum speed is $\omega a = 4 \times \frac{\pi}{4}$

$= \pi$ cm s^{-1}

(b) Maximum magnitude of acceleration

is $\omega^2 a = \left(\frac{\pi}{4}\right)^2 \times 4 = \frac{\pi^2}{4}$ cm

(c) when $x = 2$, using $v^2 = \omega^2(a^2 - x^2)$

$\Rightarrow v^2 = \frac{\pi^2}{16}(16 - 4) = \frac{\pi^2}{16}(12)$

$\Rightarrow v = \frac{\pi\sqrt{3}}{2}$ cm s^{-1}

7

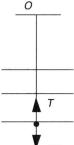

Resolving vertically
$T - mg = 0$

$\Rightarrow T = mg$ $\qquad$ ①

But $T = \frac{\lambda x}{l} = \frac{\lambda a}{l}$ $\qquad$ ②

From ① and ②,

$\frac{\lambda a}{l} = mg \Rightarrow \lambda = \frac{mgl}{a}$

$F = mf \Rightarrow T - mg = -mf$ $\qquad$ ①

using f for acceleration(minus since against the direction of x increasing)

$T = \frac{\lambda(\text{Ext})}{l} = \frac{\lambda(a + x)}{l}$

But $\lambda = \frac{mgl}{a}$

$\Rightarrow T = \frac{mgl(a + x)}{al} = \frac{mg(a + x)}{a}$ $\qquad$ ②

② into ① $\Rightarrow \frac{mg(a + x)}{a} - mg = -mf$

$\times$ by a $\quad mg(a + x) - mga = -maf$

$mga + mgx - mga = -maf$

$\Rightarrow -maf = mgx \Rightarrow f = -\frac{g}{a} x$

i.e. we have simple harmonic motion, since it is proportional to distance,

with $\omega^2 = \frac{g}{a}$

$\Rightarrow \omega = \sqrt{\frac{g}{a}}$

Using $T = \frac{2\pi}{\omega} \Rightarrow$ period is $\frac{2\pi}{\sqrt{\frac{g}{a}}} = 2\pi \sqrt{\frac{a}{g}}$

8

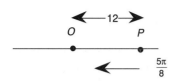

Given that when $t = 4$, $x = 12$ and $v = -\frac{5\pi}{8}$ (since moving towards O)

Also, period $T = \frac{2\pi}{\omega} = 16 \Rightarrow \omega = \frac{\pi}{8}$

Given that $x = a \cos(\omega t + \phi)$ and using $x = 12$, $t = 4$, gives

$12 = a \cos(4\omega + \phi) = a \cos\left(\phi + \frac{\pi}{2}\right)$ ... ①

$v = \frac{dx}{dt} = -a\omega \sin(\omega t + \phi)$ and using

$v = -\frac{5\pi}{8}$, $t = 4$, $\omega = \frac{\pi}{8}$

$-\frac{5\pi}{8} = -\frac{a\pi}{8} \sin\left(\phi + \frac{\pi}{2}\right)$

$\Rightarrow 5 = a \sin\left(\phi + \frac{\pi}{2}\right)$ ... ②

If we square ① and ② and add,

$12^2 + 5^2 = a^2 \cos^2\left(\phi + \frac{\pi}{2}\right) + a^2 \sin^2\left(\phi + \frac{\pi}{2}\right)$

$144 + 25 = a^2 \left(\cos^2\left(\phi + \frac{\pi}{2}\right) + \sin^2\left(\phi + \frac{\pi}{2}\right)\right)$

$\Rightarrow 169 = a^2$ since $\cos^2 + \sin^2 = 1$

$\Rightarrow a = 13$ since $a > 0$

Putting this into ①, $12 = 13 \cos\left(\phi + \frac{\pi}{2}\right)$

$\Rightarrow \frac{12}{13} = \cos\left(\phi + \frac{\pi}{2}\right)$

$0.395 = \phi + \frac{\pi}{2} \Rightarrow \phi = -1.18$

9 Given that $a = 2$ and $T = \frac{2\pi}{\omega} = 10 \Rightarrow \omega = \frac{\omega}{5}$

Maximum speed is $\omega a = \frac{2\pi}{5}$

$v = ...$ Particle starts from rest, so we can say it must be at one extreme, say $x = a$.
Putting this and $t = 0$ into $x = a \sin(\omega t + c)$
gives $a = a \sin c \Rightarrow c = \frac{\pi}{2}$,

i.e. $x = a \sin\left(\omega t + \frac{\pi}{2}\right)$

This gives $v = a\omega \cos\left(\omega t + \frac{\pi}{2}\right)$ and so

when $v = \frac{-\pi}{5}$ (since particle is moving towards the origin)

$\frac{-\pi}{5} = 2 \times \frac{\pi}{5} \cos\left(\frac{\pi}{5}t + \frac{\pi}{2}\right)$

$\Rightarrow \cos\left(\frac{\pi}{5}t + \frac{\pi}{2}\right) = -\frac{1}{2}$

$\Rightarrow \frac{\pi}{5}t + \frac{\pi}{2} = \frac{2\pi}{3}$

$\frac{\pi}{5}t = \frac{\pi}{6} \Rightarrow t = \frac{5}{6}$ s

Acceleration is $-\omega^2 x$, maximum magnitude of $\left(\frac{\pi}{5}\right)^2 \times 2$

Since $F = ma$, maximum magnitude of force is $4 \times \left(\frac{\pi}{5}\right)^2 \times 2 = \frac{8\pi^2}{25}$

10 (a) The average of the depths of water is 7 m, and so the amplitude $a = 3$ m. Time for half a cycle is $6\frac{1}{3}$ hours $= \frac{19}{3}$ hours.

$\Rightarrow \frac{1}{2}T = \frac{\pi}{\omega} = \frac{19}{3} \Rightarrow \omega = \frac{3\pi}{19}$.

We want $x = -3$ when $t = 0$ and $x = 3$ when $t = \frac{19}{3}$

where x is height above 7 m and t is time after 1100 hours.

Using $x = a \sin(\omega t + c)$ and substituting $x = -3$ when $t = 0$, $a = 3$

$-3 = 3\sin c \Rightarrow \sin c = -1 \Rightarrow c = \frac{3\pi}{2}$

i.e. $x = 3\sin\left(\frac{3\pi t}{19} + \frac{3\pi}{2}\right)$ ... ①

$\Rightarrow v = \frac{dx}{dt} = \frac{9\pi}{19} \cos\left(\frac{3\pi t}{19} + \frac{3\pi}{2}\right)$ ... ②

At 1235, i.e. $t = 1\frac{7}{12} = \frac{19}{12}$

$\Rightarrow v = \frac{9\pi}{19} \cos\left(\frac{\pi}{4} + \frac{3\pi}{2}\right) = \frac{9\pi}{19\sqrt{2}}$ m h^{-1}

(b) From ①, $x = 3\sin\left(\frac{3\pi t}{19} + \frac{3\pi}{2}\right)$

when $x = \frac{3}{2}$ (above 7 m)

$\frac{3}{2} = 3 \sin\left(\frac{3\pi t}{19} + \frac{3\pi}{2}\right)$

$\frac{1}{2} = \sin\left(\frac{3\pi t}{19} + \frac{3\pi}{2}\right)$

$\Rightarrow \frac{3\pi t}{19} + \frac{3\pi}{2} = \frac{\pi}{6}$ or $\frac{5\pi}{6}$ or $\frac{13\pi}{6}$ or ...

The first of these to give a positive answer is $\frac{13\pi}{6}$, i.e.

$\frac{3\pi t}{19} + \frac{3\pi}{2} = \frac{13\pi}{6} \Rightarrow \frac{3\pi t}{19} = \frac{2\pi}{3}$

$\Rightarrow t = \frac{38}{9} = 4$ hours 13 minutes

$\therefore$ The time will be 1513 hours.

11 (a) We can use the same argument as in question 7 to show that the period is

$2\pi\sqrt{\frac{a}{g}} \Rightarrow \omega = \sqrt{\frac{g}{a}}$

Since a is the extension produced by the weight, in this case Mg, and we are given that $a = 0.2$

$\Rightarrow \omega = \sqrt{\frac{9.8}{0.2}} = \sqrt{49} = 7$

and the period is $\frac{2\pi}{7}$

(b) (i) When at a distance x from 0, acceleration is $-\omega^2 x$ and the speed is $\omega\sqrt{a^2 - x^2}$.

When $x = 3$, $\omega^2 x = \omega\sqrt{a^2 - x^2}$

$\Rightarrow 3\omega = \sqrt{a^2 - 9}$ ... ①

Also the maximum speed, $\omega a = 2$ ... ②

$\omega = \frac{2}{a}$ into ① gives $\frac{6}{a} = \sqrt{a^2 - 9}$

$\Rightarrow \frac{36}{a^2} = a^2 - 9$ by squaring

$36 = a^4 - 9a^2 \Rightarrow a^4 - 9a^2 - 36 = 0$

$(a^2 - 12)(a^2 + 3) = 0$

$\Rightarrow a^2 = 12 \ (a^2 + 3 = 0 \text{ not possible})$

$\Rightarrow a = \sqrt{12} = 2\sqrt{3}$ (since $a > 0$)

Putting this into ②, $\omega \times 2\sqrt{3} = 2 \Rightarrow \omega = \frac{1}{\sqrt{3}}$

Period, $t = \frac{2\pi}{\omega} = 2\sqrt{3}\,\pi$

(ii) Denoting x_A the distance of A from O

$x_A = a \sin(\omega t + c)$ Putting $x_A = 2\sqrt{3}$

when $t = 0$, and $\omega = \frac{1}{\sqrt{3}}$

$\Rightarrow 2\sqrt{3} = 2\sqrt{3} \sin c$

$\Rightarrow \sin c = 1$

$c = \frac{\pi}{2}$

$\Rightarrow x_A = 2\sqrt{3} \sin\left(\frac{t}{\sqrt{3}} + \frac{\pi}{2}\right)$ ... ③

$x_B = a \sin(\omega t + c)$

$x_B = 2\sqrt{3}$ when $t = \frac{\sqrt{3}}{2}\pi$

$\Rightarrow 2\sqrt{3} = 2\sqrt{3} \sin\left(\frac{\pi}{2} + c\right)$

$\Rightarrow \sin\left(\frac{\pi}{2} + c\right) = 1 \Rightarrow c = 0$

$\Rightarrow x_B = 2\sqrt{3} \sin\left(\frac{t}{\sqrt{3}}\right)$ ... ④

Putting $x_A = x_B$ gives

$2\sqrt{3} \sin\left(\frac{t}{\sqrt{3}} + \frac{\pi}{2}\right) = 2\sqrt{3} \sin\left(\frac{t}{\sqrt{3}}\right)$

$\sin\left(\frac{t}{\sqrt{3}} + \frac{\pi}{2}\right) = \sin\left(\frac{t}{\sqrt{3}}\right)$

But $\sin\left(\frac{t}{\sqrt{3}}\right) = \sin\left(\pi - \frac{t}{\sqrt{3}}\right)$ or $\sin\left(3\pi - \frac{t}{\sqrt{3}}\right)$

$\Rightarrow \frac{t}{\sqrt{3}} + \frac{\pi}{2} = \pi - \frac{t}{\sqrt{3}}$ or $\frac{t}{\sqrt{3}} + \frac{\pi}{2} = 3\pi - \frac{t}{\sqrt{3}}$

$t = \frac{\sqrt{3}}{4}\pi$ or $t = \frac{5\sqrt{3}}{4}\pi$

The first solution is before B is released, so we discard.

The second solution is

$\frac{5\sqrt{3}}{4}\pi - \frac{\sqrt{3}}{2}\pi = \frac{3\sqrt{3}}{4}\pi$ after release of B.

The distance from O is given by

$\left| 2\sqrt{3} \sin\left(\frac{5\sqrt{3}}{4}\pi \times \frac{1}{\sqrt{3}}\right) \right|$

$= \left| 2\sqrt{3} \sin\frac{5\pi}{4} \right| = \left| \frac{-2\sqrt{3}}{\sqrt{2}} \right| = 2\sqrt{\frac{3}{2}}$

since distance > 0

Section 6

1

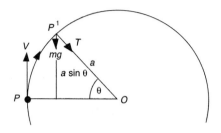

We have a different starting point and so our two equations are not quite the same.

Taking the zero potential level to be the horizontal through O,

Conservation of energy:

$$\frac{1}{2}mV^2 = \frac{1}{2}mv^2 + mga\sin\theta \qquad \dots \text{①}$$

where v is the velocity at P^1.

Circular motion: $T + mg\sin\theta = \dfrac{mv^2}{a} \qquad \dots \text{②}$

From ①, $mv^2 = mV^2 - 2mga\sin\theta$ and putting this into ②

$$T + mg\sin\theta = \frac{mV^2}{a} - 2mg\sin\theta$$

i.e. $T = \dfrac{mV^2}{a} - 3mg\sin\theta \qquad \dots \text{③}$

We need $T \geq 0$ for complete circles, i.e.

$$\frac{mv^2}{a} \geq 3mg\sin\theta$$

$$v^2 \geq 3ag\sin\theta$$

The tension will be least at the top of the circle, i.e. $\theta = 90°$.

so we need $v^2 \geq 3ag\sin 90°$

$$\geq 3ag \implies v \geq \sqrt{3ag}$$

(a) Putting $T = \dfrac{15mg}{2}$ and $V = \sqrt{6ag}$ into ③,

$$\frac{15mg}{2} = \frac{m \times 6ag}{a} - 3mg\sin\theta$$

i.e. $3mg\sin\theta = 6mg - \dfrac{15mg}{2} = -\dfrac{3mg}{2}$

$$\implies \sin\theta = -\frac{1}{2}$$

The string will break when the particle has passed the horizontal on the other side, i.e. when $\theta = 210°$

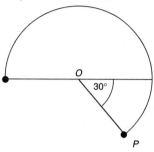

so the angle that OP makes with the *vertical* is $60°$

(b) The greatest tension is at the bottom of the circle, when $\theta = 270°$ and $\sin\theta = -1$.

Putting $T = \dfrac{15mg}{2}$ and $\sin\theta = -1$ into ③,

$$\frac{15mg}{2} = \frac{mV^2}{a} + 3mg$$

$$\frac{9mg}{2} = \frac{mV^2}{a} \implies V^2 = \frac{9ag}{2}$$

and $V = \sqrt{\dfrac{9ag}{2}}$

2   By conservation of energy, taking the zero potential energy level to be the bottom of the circle

At the top: KE is $\frac{1}{2}mV^2$ PE is $mg\,2a$

At the bottom: KE is $\frac{1}{2}mv^2$ PE is 0

Equating the sums of these

$$\frac{1}{2}mv^2 = \frac{1}{2}mV^2 + 2mga$$

$$v^2 = V^2 + 4ag \implies v = \sqrt{V^2 + 4ag}$$

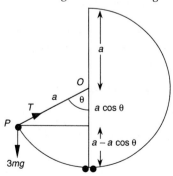

On collision, by conservation of momentum,

$$mv = 3mv' \Rightarrow v' = \frac{v}{3} = \frac{1}{3}\sqrt{V^2 + 4ag}$$

where v' is the speed after the collision.

Now the kinetic energy at bottom is

$$\frac{1}{2} \times 3m \times (v')^2 = \frac{1}{2} \times 3m \times \frac{1}{9}(V^2 + 4ag)$$

Potential energy at P is

$$3m \times g \times a(1 - \cos\theta)$$

and if we call the speed U, the kinetic energy will be $\frac{1}{2} \times 3m \times U^2$.

Equating the sums of the energies at these two points,

$$\frac{1}{2} \times 3m \times \frac{1}{9}(V^2 + 4ag)$$

$$= 3m \times g \times a(1 - \cos\theta) + \frac{1}{2} \times 3m \times U^2$$

$$\Rightarrow \frac{1}{2}U^2 = \frac{1}{18}(V^2 + 4ag) - ag(1 - \cos\theta) \quad \dots \text{①}$$

The force inwards at P is $T - 3mg\cos\theta$, and since the motion is circular, this must be $\dfrac{3m \times U^2}{a}$

$$T - 3mg\cos\theta = \frac{3m}{a}U^2$$

$$= \frac{3m}{a} \times 2\left[\frac{1}{18}(V^2 + 4ag) - ag(1 - \cos\theta)\right]$$

$$= \frac{m}{3a}(V^2 + 4ag) - 6mg + 6mg\cos\theta$$

$$\Rightarrow T = \frac{mV^2}{3a} + \frac{4mg}{3} - 6mg + 6mg\cos\theta$$

$$+ 3mg\cos\theta$$

$$= \frac{mV^2}{3a} - \frac{14mg}{3} + 9mg\cos\theta$$

For complete circles, we need $T \geq 0$ when $\theta = 180°$, i.e. at the top of the circle. This condition is

$$\frac{mV^2}{3a} - \frac{14mg}{3} + 9mg\cos\theta \geq 0$$

$$\cos 180° = -1$$

$$\frac{V^2}{3a} - \frac{14g}{3} - 9g \geq 0 \Rightarrow \frac{V^2}{3a} > \frac{41g}{3}$$

$$\Rightarrow V^2 \geq 41ag$$

$$\Rightarrow V \geq \sqrt{41ag}$$

3 The minimum tension occurs when the particle is at the highest point of the vertical circle.

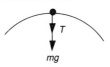

At this point, the force towards the centre is

$$T + mg = 3mg + mg = 4mg \qquad \dots \text{①}$$

Initially the KE was $\frac{1}{2}mu^2$

At the top, the PE is $mg \times 2a$,

and the KE is $\frac{1}{2}mv^2$

By conservation of energy,

$$\frac{1}{2}mu^2 = \frac{1}{2}mv^2 + 2mga \Rightarrow v^2 = u^2 - 4ga$$

But force towards centre is

$$\frac{mv^2}{a} = \frac{m(u^2 - 4ga)}{a} \qquad \dots \text{②}$$

Equating ① and ②, $4mg = \dfrac{m(u^2 - 4ga)}{a}$

$$4ma = mu^2 - 4mga$$

$$\Rightarrow u^2 = 8ga \Rightarrow u = \sqrt{8ga}$$

(a)

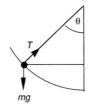

We have from energy,

$$\frac{1}{2}mu^2 = \frac{1}{2}mv^2 + mga(1 - \cos\theta)$$

i.e. $8ga = v^2 + 2ga(1 - \cos\theta)$

$$\Rightarrow v^2 = 6ga + 2ga\cos\theta \qquad \dots \text{③}$$

Force inwards,

$$T - mg\cos\theta = \frac{mv^2}{a}$$

$$= \frac{6mga + 2mga\cos\theta}{a}$$

$$\Rightarrow T = 6mg + 3mg\cos\theta \qquad \dots \text{④}$$

(b) Horizontal force is :

$T \sin \theta = 6mg \sin \theta + 3mg \sin \theta \cos \theta$

since opposes motion, horizontal component is $-3g \sin \theta (2 + \cos \theta)$

Vertical force is :

$T \cos \theta - mg = 6mg \cos \theta + 3mg \cos^2 \theta - mg$

i.e. vertical component of acceleration is $6g \cos \theta + 3g \cos^2 \theta - g$

4

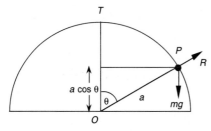

Suppose the hemisphere has a radius of a. Then the particle at the later position is $a - a \cos \theta$ below the initial position.

Energies: $0 = \frac{1}{2} mv^2 - mga (1 - \cos \theta)$ ... ①

Circular motion: $mg \cos \theta - R = \frac{mv^2}{a}$ ... ②

$\Rightarrow R = mg \cos \theta - \frac{mv^2}{a}$

$\quad = mg \cos \theta - 2 mg (1 - \cos \theta)$ from ②

$\quad = 3 mg \cos \theta - 2 mg$

$\quad = mg (3 \cos \theta - 2)$

This leaves the surface of the sphere, i.e. $R = 0$, when $mg (3 \cos \theta - 2) = 0$

$\Rightarrow 3 \cos \theta = 2 \Rightarrow \theta = \cos^{-1} \frac{2}{3}$

5   The first part is covered in the text (see the Example on p. 93).

If $V = 2\sqrt{ag}$ at the bottom, the KE is $\frac{1}{2} m(4ag)$

When the string is horizontal, the PE is mga.

The KE is then $\frac{1}{2} m(4ag) - mga = \frac{1}{2} mv^2$

$\Rightarrow v^2 = 2ag$.

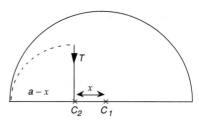

At the top of the circle, gain in PE is $mg(a - x)$.

If velocity is v', KE is $\frac{1}{2} m(v')^2$ and we have

$\frac{1}{2} m(2ag) = mg(a - x) + \frac{1}{2} m(v')^2$ ...①

Also, $T + mg = \dfrac{mv'^2}{(a - x)}$

Minimum when $T = 0$

$\Rightarrow (v')^2 = (a - x)g$

Into ① gives

$mag = mag - mgx + \frac{1}{2} mag - \frac{1}{2} mxg$

$\Rightarrow \frac{3}{2} mgx = \frac{1}{2} mga$

$\Rightarrow x = \frac{1}{3} a$ from the centre

6

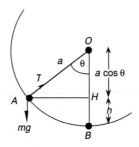

Energies: If the initial position is taken as the zero potential level, the initial sum of energies is:

$\frac{1}{2} mV^2$ $(+ 0)$

when OA makes an angle θ with the downwards vertical, the vertical height h of A above B is $a - a \cos \theta = a (1 - \cos \theta)$. If the velocity is taken to be v, the new sum of energies is:

$\frac{1}{2} mv^2 = mga (1 - \cos \theta)$

Equating these two sums gives

$$\frac{1}{2}mV^2 = \frac{1}{2}mv^2 + mga\,(1 - \cos\theta) \qquad \ldots \textcircled{1}$$

When the particle is vertically above O,

$\theta = 180° \Rightarrow \cos\theta = -1$ and $\textcircled{1}$ becomes

$$\frac{1}{2}mV^2 = \frac{1}{2}mv^2 + 2mga$$

$$\Rightarrow v^2 = V^2 - 4ag$$

$$\Rightarrow v = \sqrt{V^2 - 4ag} \qquad \ldots \textcircled{2}$$

Circular motion: Resolving towards the centre gives:

$$T - mg\cos\theta = \frac{mv^2}{a} \qquad \ldots \textcircled{3}$$

and combining $\textcircled{2}$ and $\textcircled{3}$

$$T = m\frac{(V^2 - 4ag)}{a} + mg\cos\theta$$

We need $T > 0$ when $\theta = 180°$,

i.e. $\cos\theta = -1$ for complete circles,

$$\Rightarrow \frac{m(V^2 - 4ag)}{a} - mg > 0$$

$$V^2 - 4ag > ag$$

$$V^2 > 5ag$$

$$V > \sqrt{5ag}$$

For the collision, by conservation of momentum $mv = 2mv'$ where v' is the velocity of the composite particle and so:

$$v' = \frac{1}{2}v = \frac{1}{2}\sqrt{V^2 - 4ag}$$

i.e. the speed of the particle is halved when it picks up the second particle.

At the instant of collision, the tension, which will be a minimum, is given by the circular motion equation for the composite particle.

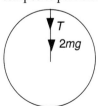

$$T + 2mg = \frac{2mv^2}{a} \qquad \ldots \textcircled{4}$$

(noting that the mass is now doubled)

i.e. $$T = \frac{2mv^2}{a} - 2mg$$

$$= \frac{2m}{a}\left[\frac{1}{2}\sqrt{V^2 - 4ag}\,\right]^2 - 2mg$$

$$= \frac{2m}{a} \times \frac{1}{4} \times (V^2 - 4ag) - 2mg$$

$$= \frac{mV^2}{2a} - 2mg - 2mg$$

$$= \frac{mV^2}{2a} - 4mg \qquad \ldots \textcircled{5}$$

Since we require $T \geq 0$, $\dfrac{mV^2}{2a} - 4mg \geq 0$

$$\Rightarrow \frac{mV^2}{2a} \geq 4mg \Rightarrow V^2 \geq 8ag$$

and least value of V is $\sqrt{8ag}$

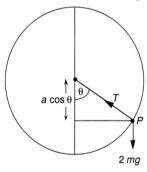

Relative to the top, the composite particle has lost $2mg\,(a + a\cos\theta)$ in potential energy. If we call the new velocity V', it has gained

$$\frac{1}{2} \times 2m \times v^2 - \frac{1}{2} \times 2m \times V'^2$$

i.e. $m[v - V'^2]$ in kinetic energy.

Then $\qquad m[v^2 - V'^2] = 2mga(1 + \cos\theta)$

and since $\quad V'^2 = \frac{1}{4}(V^2 - 4ag)$,

$$v^2 - \frac{1}{4}V^2 + ag = 2ag + 2ag\cos\theta$$

$$\Rightarrow v^2 = \frac{1}{4}V^2 + ag(1 + 2\cos\theta) \qquad \ldots \textcircled{6}$$

Our circular motion equation is

$$T - 2mg\cos\theta = \frac{2mv^2}{a} \qquad \ldots \textcircled{7}$$

Combining these,

$$T - 2mg \cos \theta = \frac{2m}{a} \left[\frac{1}{4}V^2 + ag(1 + 2 \cos \theta) \right]$$

$$T - 2mg \cos \theta = \frac{mV^2}{2a} + 2mg + 4mg \cos \theta$$

$$T = \frac{mV^2}{2a} + 2mg + 6mg \cos \theta$$

(As a check for this, note that if $T = 0$ and $\cos \theta = -1$, $V^2 = 8ag$ which is the result we showed previously.)

Section 7

1

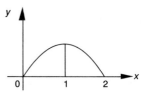

The shape is symmetrical about the maximum point, i.e. $x = 1$, and so $\bar{x} = 1$.

The y-coordinate of the centre of mass is given by

$$\bar{y} = \frac{\frac{1}{2} \displaystyle\int y^2 \, dx}{\displaystyle\int y \, dx} = \frac{\frac{1}{2} \displaystyle\int_0^2 \left(2x - x^2\right)^2 \, dx}{\displaystyle\int_0^2 \left(2x - x^2\right) \, dx}$$

$$= \frac{\frac{1}{2} \displaystyle\int_0^2 \left(4x^2 - 4x^3 + x^4\right) \, dx}{\displaystyle\int_0^2 \left(2x - x^2\right) \, dx}$$

$$= \frac{\frac{1}{2} \left[\dfrac{4x^3}{3} - x^4 + \dfrac{x^5}{5} \right]_0^2}{\left[x^2 - \dfrac{x^3}{3} \right]_0^2}$$

$$= \frac{\frac{1}{2} \left(\frac{32}{3} - 16 + \frac{32}{5} \right)}{\frac{4}{3}} = \frac{\frac{8}{15}}{\frac{4}{3}} = \frac{2}{5}$$

The required coordinates are $\left(1, \frac{2}{5}\right)$.

2 Since the x-axis is an axis of symmetry, $\bar{y} = 0$

$$\bar{x} = \frac{\int xy^2 \, dx}{\int y^2 \, dx} = \frac{\displaystyle\int_0^1 x(x^2 + 1)^2 \, dx}{\displaystyle\int_0^1 (x^2 + 1)^2 \, dx}$$

$$= \frac{\displaystyle\int_0^1 (x^5 + 2x^3 + x) \, dx}{\displaystyle\int_0^1 (x^4 + 2x^2 + 1) \, dx}$$

$$= \frac{\left[\frac{x^6}{6} + \frac{x^4}{2} + \frac{x^2}{2} \right]_0^1}{\left[\frac{x^5}{5} + \frac{2x^3}{3} + x \right]_0^1}$$

$$= \frac{\frac{7}{6}}{\frac{28}{15}} = \frac{5}{8} \text{ , i.e. coordinates are } \left(\frac{5}{8}, 0 \right)$$

3 Moments about AD, assuming ρ is the mass per unit, are:

	Vol	Mass	CoM	Moment
Big cube	$27a^3$	$27a^3\rho$	$\frac{3a}{2}$	$\frac{81a^4\rho}{2}$
Medium cube	$8a^3$	$8a^3\rho$	$2a$	$16a^4\rho$
Little cube	a^3	$a^3\rho$	$\frac{3a}{2}$	$\frac{3a^4\rho}{2}$
Whole	$36a^3$	$36a^3\rho$	$\bar{x}$	$36a^3\rho\bar{x}$

Equating, $36a^3\rho\bar{x} = \frac{81a^4\rho}{2} + 16a^4\rho + \frac{3a^4\rho}{2}$

$$= \left(\frac{81 + 32 + 3}{2} \right) a^4\rho = \frac{116a^4\rho}{2}$$

$$\bar{x} = \frac{116a^4\rho}{2} \times \frac{1}{36a^3\rho} = \frac{29a}{18}$$

Moments about AB:

	Mass	CoM	Moment
Big	$27a^3\rho$	$\frac{3a}{2}$	$\frac{81a^4\rho}{2}$
Medium	$8a^3\rho$	$4a$	$32a^4\rho$
Little	$a^3\rho$	$\frac{11a}{2}$	$\frac{11a^4\rho}{2}$
Whole	$36a^3\rho$	$\bar{y}$	$36a^3\rho y$

Equating, $36a^3\rho\bar{y} = \frac{a^4\rho}{2} [81 + 64 + 11]$

$$\Rightarrow \bar{y} = \frac{39a}{18}$$

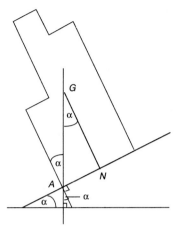

If G is the position of the centre of mass and N the foot of the perpendicular from G on to AB, then $GN = \frac{39a}{18}$ and $AN = \frac{29a}{18}$

$$\Rightarrow \tan \alpha = \frac{AN}{GN} = \frac{\frac{29a}{18}}{\frac{39a}{18}} = \frac{29}{39}$$

4 The first part is standard proof (see p. 113)

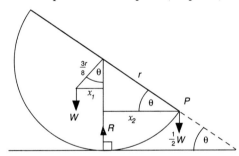

Taking moments about the vertical axis through the point of contact,

$$Wx_1 = \frac{1}{2} Wx_2 \qquad \qquad \dots①$$

from small Δ, $x_1 = \frac{3r}{8} \sin \theta \qquad \dots②$

from large Δ, $x_2 = r \cos \theta \qquad \dots③$

② and ③ into ①, $\frac{3r}{8} \sin \theta = \frac{r}{2} \cos \theta$

$$\Rightarrow \tan \theta = \frac{4}{3}$$

5 The first part is a standard proof (see p. 112).

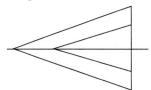

Moments about vertical axis through vertex

$$\frac{1}{3}\pi a^2 h\rho \times \frac{3h}{4} - \frac{1}{3}\pi \left(\frac{a}{2}\right)^2 \left(\frac{2}{3}h\right)\rho \times \frac{5h}{6}$$

$$= \left[\frac{1}{3}\pi a^2 h\rho - \frac{1}{3}\pi \left(\frac{a}{2}\right)^2 \left(\frac{2h}{3}\right)\rho \right]\bar{x}$$

$$\Rightarrow \pi a^2 h^2 \rho \left[\frac{1}{4} - \frac{5}{108}\right]$$

$$= \pi a^2 h\rho \left[\frac{1}{3} - \frac{1}{18}\right] \times \bar{x}$$

$$\Rightarrow \bar{x} = \frac{11}{15}h$$

6 Moments about axis through O,

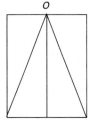

$$\pi r^2 h\rho \times \frac{h}{2} - \frac{1}{3}\pi r^2 h\rho \times \frac{3h}{4} = \frac{2}{3}\pi r^2 h\rho \bar{y}$$

$$\Rightarrow \frac{\pi r^2 h^2}{4} = \frac{2}{3}\pi r^2 h\bar{y}$$

$$\Rightarrow \bar{y} = \frac{3h}{8}$$

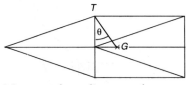

Moments about diameter of common face, right being positive

$$-\frac{1}{3}\pi r^2 h\rho \times \frac{h}{4} + \frac{2}{3}r^2 h\rho \times \frac{3h}{8} = \pi r^2 h\bar{x}$$

$$\Rightarrow \bar{x} = \frac{h}{6}$$

Angle TG to vertical is same as axis to horizontal

$$\tan \theta = \frac{\frac{h}{6}}{r} = \frac{1}{3} \text{ since } h = \frac{r}{2}$$

7 (a) The first part is a standard proof which is covered at the beginning of this section.

(b)

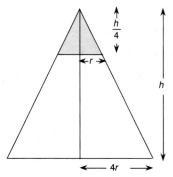

By similar triangles, the radius of the cone removed is going to be r.

Moment whole =
    Moment remainder + Moment part

Taking moments about the base

$$\left(\frac{1}{3}\pi (4r)^2 h\right) \times \frac{h}{4}$$

$$= \left[\frac{1}{3}\pi (4r)^2 h - \frac{1}{3}\pi (r)^2 \left(\frac{h}{4}\right)\right]\bar{y} + \frac{1}{3}\pi r^2 \frac{h}{4}$$

$$\times \left(\frac{3h}{4} + \frac{h}{16}\right)$$

$$\frac{4\pi r^2 h^2}{3} = \frac{1}{3}\pi r^2 h \left(\frac{63}{4}\right)\bar{y} + \frac{13\pi r^2 h^2}{192}$$

$$\Rightarrow \frac{1}{3}\pi r^2 h \left(\frac{63}{4}\right)\bar{y} = \frac{4\pi r^2 h^2}{3} - \frac{13\pi r^2 h^2}{192}$$

$$= \frac{81\pi r^2 h^2}{64}$$

$$\Rightarrow \bar{y} = \frac{4}{21} \times \frac{81}{64}h = \frac{27h}{112}$$

(c)

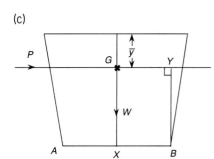

If the force is pushing towards the right, the frustum is going to tip about the point B. This will happen basically when the force overcomes the weight: more precisely when the moment of the force about B is greater than the moment of the weight about B, i.e. when

$$P \times BY > W \times BX \qquad \dots \text{①}$$

Since the height of the frustum is $\frac{3}{4}h$ and $\bar{y}$ is $\frac{27h}{112}$, $BY = \frac{3}{4}h - \frac{27h}{112} = \frac{57h}{112} = \frac{57(6r)}{112}$ (given)

$BX = r$, which means ① becomes

$$P \times \frac{57(6r)}{112} > Wr$$

i.e. $P > \dfrac{56W}{171}$

8

Moments about OA:

$$3a\rho \times \frac{3a}{2} + 2a\rho \times 3a = 9a\rho\bar{x}$$

$$\Rightarrow \frac{21a\rho}{2} = 9a\rho\bar{x} \Rightarrow \bar{x} = \frac{7a}{6}$$

Moments about ON:

$$4a\rho \times 2a + 2a\rho \times a = 9a\bar{y}$$

$$\Rightarrow \bar{y} = \frac{10a}{9}$$

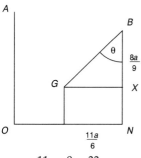

$$\tan\theta = \frac{11}{6} \times \frac{9}{8} = \frac{33}{16}$$

9

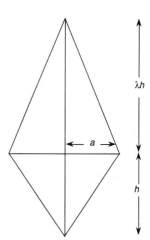

Taking moments about their base, with distances above the base taken as positive gives

Moment whole = Moment large + Moment small

$$\left(\frac{1}{3}\pi r^2\lambda h + \frac{1}{3}\pi r^2 h\right)\bar{y}$$

$$= \frac{1}{3}\pi r^2(\lambda h) \times \frac{\lambda h}{4} - \frac{1}{3}\pi r^2 h \times \frac{h}{4}$$

$$\Rightarrow \frac{1}{3}\pi r^2 h(\lambda + 1)\bar{y} = \frac{1}{3}\pi r^2 \frac{h^2}{4}(\lambda^2 - 1)$$

$$\bar{y} = \frac{h}{4}\left(\frac{\lambda^2 - 1}{\lambda + 1}\right) = \frac{h}{4}(\lambda - 1)$$

Required distance, from top of figure, is

$$\lambda h - \bar{y} = \lambda h - \frac{\lambda h}{4} + \frac{h}{4} = \frac{h}{4}(3\lambda + 1)$$

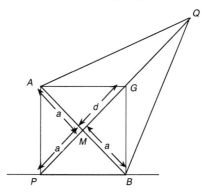

ABP represents the smaller cone in contact with a horizontal surface.

Since $MB = MP = a$,

$M\hat{B}P = M\hat{A}P = 45°$ and $A\hat{P}B = 90°$

In the limiting position G, the position of the centre of mass of the composite figure, is directly above B, i.e. GB is vertical

$\Rightarrow G\hat{B}M = 45°$, i.e. $d = a$.

But we know that $d = \bar{y}$ which we found above, i.e. $d = \frac{h}{4}(\lambda - 1)$. Putting $d = a = h$ into this gives $a = \frac{a}{4}(\lambda - 1)$

$\Rightarrow \lambda - 1 = 4 \Rightarrow \lambda = 5$

This is the limiting position: equilibrium is possible for any value of λ, $\lambda \le 5$.

10

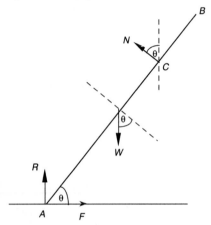

We want to find N, and for now are not interested in the forces acting on the lower part of the rod, so we take moments about A.

$A\,\rotatebox{-45}{$\downarrow$}$: $2a\,W\cos\theta - 3aN = 0$

$\Rightarrow N = \frac{2}{3}W\cos\theta$

We can now simply look at all the vertical forces acting on the rod

$N\cos\theta + R - W = 0 \Rightarrow R = W - \frac{2}{3}W\cos^2\theta$

$= W\left(1 - \frac{2}{3}\cos^2\theta\right)$

And at the horizontal forces acting on the rod

$F - N\sin\theta = 0$

$\Rightarrow F = N\sin\theta = \frac{2}{3}W\cos\theta\sin\theta$

$= \frac{W\sin 2\theta}{3}$

Since the maximum value of F is μR,

i.e. $F \le \mu R \Rightarrow \mu \ge \frac{F}{R}$

$= \dfrac{\dfrac{W\sin 2\theta}{3}}{W\left(1 - \dfrac{2}{3}\cos^2\theta\right)}$

$= \dfrac{\sin 2\theta}{3 - 2\cos^2\theta}$

But $\cos 2\theta = 2\cos^2\theta - 1$

$\Rightarrow 2\cos^2\theta = \cos 2\theta + 1$

$\Rightarrow \mu \ge \dfrac{\sin 2\theta}{3 - (\cos 2\theta + 1)}$

$\Rightarrow \mu \ge \dfrac{\sin 2\theta}{2 - \cos 2\theta}$

11

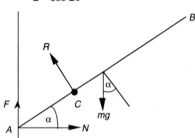

The first thing is to draw a diagram with all the forces acting on the rod.

Since the rail is smooth, the reaction will be at right-angles to the rod. We are not told that the friction is limiting, at the wall, so we put the frictional force as F rather than μN.

Taking moments about A,

$R \times \lambda l - mg\cos\alpha \times l = 0$

$\Rightarrow R = \dfrac{mg\cos\alpha}{\lambda}$ ... ①

Looking at the vertical forces acting on the rod,

$F + R\cos\alpha = mg \Rightarrow F = mg - R\cos\alpha$

But $F > 0$ (given) $\Rightarrow mg - R\cos\alpha > 0$

$\Rightarrow mg - \dfrac{mg\cos^2\alpha}{\lambda} > 0$ putting in ①

$mg > \dfrac{mg\cos^2\alpha}{\lambda} \Rightarrow \lambda > \cos^2\alpha$